D1276438

repairers of the [breach]

a return to the discarded values of the past

repairers of the [breach]

a return to the discarded values of the past

ROD PARSLEY

RESULTS
PUBLISHING

Unless otherwise indicated, all Scripture quotations are taken from the *King James Version* of the Bible.

Repairers of the Breach
ISBN 1-933336-79-X (hardcover)
Copyright © 1993, 2007 by Rod Parsley
World Harvest Church
P.O. Box 32903
Columbus, Ohio 43232-0903

Published by:
Results Publishing
P.O. Box 32932
Columbus, Ohio 43232-0932

Contents

Dedication

I dedicate this book to my best friend – my precious wife Joni. You are the perfect helpmeet for me, hewn out of a rock by God. Thank you for helping me to fulfill the directive that God has given me to declare this message to this final generation. I thank my God upon every remembrance of you, as we stand together repairing the breach and restoring the paths to dwell in.

Foreword

I have known Rod Parsley for a number of years. In the 42 years that I have preached the gospel, I have yet to meet a man with a greater anointing and mandate from God to reach a nation.

Few men today understand what it is to preach, "Thus saith the Word of the Lord." Rod Parsley is one of those men that dare speak for God. He is a man that preaches the gospel as it is, without compromise.

It was my privilege to hear him preach the message from which this book was derived. In all my years, I have never heard a message that I feel is more needed for our generation today than *Repairers of the Breach*.

This book is more than a book. This is a message from God to the church. This is a message from God to the preachers. Repair and restore: the saving message of Jesus Christ.

I am proud to call Rod Parsley a dear friend. More importantly, I respect him as a man of God, raised up by God to preach a message from God to our dying world.

You will not be able to lay this book down until you have finished it.

Sincerely,
Dwight Thompson

Introduction

Crystal Chandeliers,
Broken Bridges

I will never forget the sacred anointing in that campmeeting service where I first had the privilege of preaching the God-given revelation message out of Isaiah 58:12 about repairing the breach and rebuilding the gospel bridge Satan has stolen from the Body of Christ.

> **"...and thou shalt be called, The repairer of the breach,**
> **The restorer of paths to dwell in."**

In that meeting, I shared how a breach – a chasm – exists between God and man, and I revealed how to span that chasm through a bridge fashioned from biblical planks. God gave breakthrough power at that campmeeting to those hearing this mighty revelation.

"You no longer need to be lonely, to feel separated from God," I told them. You no longer need to feel mangled in your marriage or oppressed at your office. God has a plan to repair every breach in your life, to span every chasm that keeps you isolated and lonely, feeling separated from Him! His Word provides you with the biblical planks you need to repair any breach in your life."

Immediately after that campmeeting service, God spoke to me in my spirit and directed me to write down the biblical revelations He had shown me. As I obeyed, He promised me that the same breakthrough anointing He gave this message at the campmeeting would flow into your life as you read these written pages!

You now hold in your hands the essence of that life-changing message!

There is great joy and anticipation in my heart to know God will honor His promise – and a new anointing will flow into your life as you experience, page by page, the campmeeting revelations God gave to me on repairing the breach.

Open your heart to receive His revolutionary message. Let the Holy Ghost deposit life-transforming seed into the fertile soil of your spirit – seed that will change you forever! I have shared my heart with you in this book because I believe this mandate of God must be delivered to our generation. I pray that as you read these pages, God will nail down each plank of His gospel bridge in your life forever.

It is God's time for you to repair every breach in your own life, to begin to build a holy bridge that will allow you to pass over into His *total* salvation, His *complete* deliverance, and His *breakthrough* power.

The gospel bridge needs to be rebuilt; and together, through the biblical principles in this book, we are going to nail down the planks and close the gaps.

The plank of salvation must be firmly fixed on the holy bridge.

When I was eight years old, I went to a Pentecostal meeting. I was a Baptist boy who liked to play cowpoke, complete with matched six-shooters, a cowboy hat to cover my burr haircut, and cowboy boots covered by blue jeans with the cuffs rolled up.

One day that cowboy entered a little cinder block church building with a 45-watt bulb on an electric cord hanging down out of the ceiling. I heard a woman preacher who had been talking in tongues.

At eight, I did not understand everything; but I knew there was something in the air. I could almost feel the cool breeze of eternity blowing around my shoulders.

Fire was there that day. When that lady preacher walked up to that little old pulpit, there was an electricity, a conviction in the air.

And so at eight years of age, I reached my trembling hand out and grabbed hold of my Mama's dress tail when the altar call came. I said, "Mama, I've got to go."

She was so surprised all she could say was "Why?" Mama knew I had been raised in the church, so I understood what she meant.

"Because I am a sinner, Mama," I replied.

Notice I did not say, "Because I want God to buy me a fancy car and ostrich shoes." I did not say, "Because I want to feel better." I just confessed that I was a sinner.

It must have been the right answer for Mama, because she just smiled at me and said, "You can go."

Only sinners need a Savior! Those who are well do not need a physician (Mark 2:17).

After that experience, no one needed a follow-up program to get me back in church. No one had to beg me to come to the next service. I was so excited about receiving Jesus that I began to take the newspaper and scour its pages, trying to find where they were having the next revival meeting.

I would tell my Mama and Daddy, "I want to go to church." They never had to tell me, "Now you are going to go to Wednesday night service whether you want to or not." Why? Because I experienced salvation, knew that my Redeemer liveth; and I wanted to be with Him.

In recent years, the church has been about the business of re-writing the unadulterated Word of God. Some divinity schools and their elitist scholars have deflated the born again, salvation experience to an insignificant speck in their philosophical dissertations.

But the Bible still says, **"Ye must be born again" (John 3:7).** That was true for me at 8 years old, and it is true for the unsaved grandfather who is 100.

I still believe in the sin-eradicating, life-changing experience provided through the sinless shed blood of a crucified carpenter from Nazareth.

The plank of healing needs to be refastened to the gospel bridge.

The Bible declares, **"with his stripes we are healed" (Isaiah 53:5),** and **"by whose stripes ye were healed" (1 Peter 2:24).** Many

11

"biblical scholars" have tried to dilute the healing power of God's Word by claiming these declarations concern spiritual, not physical healing.

That is a lie from the devil!

The Christian world at large has been fooled into thinking that the Jesus who healed blind, begging Bartimaeus is a different Jesus than the one poised majestically on the right hand of the Father interceding on our behalf. Jesus was moved with compassion to heal the sick (Matthew 14:14).

And He still is!

> **"Jesus Christ [is] the same yesterday, and to day, and for ever."**
>
> **Hebrews 13:8**

God was a healer yesterday, and He will heal today! To experience His healing nature, you must first come into His presence, prepared and expectant. The atmosphere of expectancy is the birthplace of miracles. The main reason people do not experience healing today is because no one will pray for them and expect a miracle.

No one wants to take God's Word, believe it, and apply it.

> **"And the prayer of faith shall save the sick, and the Lord shall raise him up…"**
>
> **James 5:15**

I believe in that scripture, and can personally testify about its truth.

The medical authorities gave my sister only 3 months to live, and they sent her home to die. The doctors prescribed nearly 40 different medications for her each day!

My mother was told she needed an emergency mastectomy surgery because her breast was filled with cancer.

But I have good news. James 5:15 is as true today as it was in the time of Christ! Both my mother and my sister were instantaneously made whole by one touch of the mighty healing hand of Jesus Christ.

Jesus met a man on the shores of Galilee in the country of Gadarenes possessed by a legion of demons (Luke 8:27). Shackles and chains were the only garment that clothed the wild-eyed stranger. Standing in the authority of His Heavenly Father, Jesus commanded the legion to go.

The man was instantaneously delivered from his condition!

Freedom through deliverance belongs as another plank permanently fixed to our holy bridge.

The doctrine of deliverance has been replaced by self-help groups and counseling sessions that tap dance around the root of the problem – the devil. The spoken Word of Jesus Christ had the power to drive out the forces of darkness 2,000 years ago, and the spoken Word has the same power today.

When we, the church, speak the Word of God for deliverance, the shackles and chains of bondage are destroyed.

> **"And when the day of Pentecost was fully come, they were all with one accord in one place. And suddenly there came a sound from heaven as of a rushing mighty wind, and it filled all the house where they were sitting. And there appeared unto them cloven tongues like as of fire, and it sat upon each of them. And they were all filled with the Holy Ghost, and began to speak with other tongues, as the Spirit gave them utterance."**
>
> **Acts 2:1-4**

The plank of power through the Holy Ghost has been torn from its rightful position, and must be nailed back onto the bridge.

It is my deep desire to see a powerful return to preaching on the mighty baptism in the Holy Ghost. The very doorway to the operation of the precious spiritual gifts in today's church has been slammed shut under the weight of legalism and lethargy. Many Pentecostal churches have almost banned speaking in tongues from Sunday morning services for fear of scaring off potential church-roll candidates. This wonderful river of living water has been channeled to an occasional use in Wednesday night prayer meetings and home cell groups.

I am tired of the devil waltzing around in the church, making the very elect of God feel embarrassed to display the evidence of God's presence. I want to hear the church cry out to God, "Lord, baptize us in power. Baptize us in fire. Father, give us an old-fashioned, heart-igniting baptism in the Holy Ghost!"

Samson made the mistake of believing he could do what he wanted to do, go where he wanted to go, and hear what he wanted to hear. In a crisis, he believed he needed only to go out and shake himself to overcome any enemy onslaught. But when the Philistines came, and Samson tried to shake himself, he woefully discovered that **"...the Lord was departed from him" (Judges 16:20).**

Samson, much like our modern church, was resting solely on the victories and laurels of the past. In our churches, altar calls dwindle to a minimal occurrence and healings exist only in the pages of church history journals and in the descriptions of the visiting evangelist.

The church sits idly numb, perplexed, dumbfounded – without an answer.

But God *has* given us His answer!

In the words of John Osteen, "The church has become so worldly and the world has become so churchy that it is hard to tell the difference."

There is no separation, no distinction.

In God's eyes, there are two camps: the saved and the unsaved; and He wants the dividing line clearly marked.

The church needs to place the plank of holiness back on our gospel bridge.

"Be ye holy" (1 Peter 1:16). The body of Christ must know that this plank should be nailed into its position on the bridge.

I am excited about what God is doing in these last days, but we must break down the damming walls of religious tradition.

We must refuse to coexist with compromise.

To bring about the fullness of God's end-time revival, the church must rend, purify, and sanctify its heart, glorifying the living God in all manner of prayer and praise with all boldness.

Most importantly, the gospel bridge, in its dilapidated state, must be rebuilt! Each plank must first be secured, then protected and guarded to ensure its preservation.

God is searching for a holy remnant from around the world who will repair the breach and restore the paths to dwell in.

It is my deepest desire to be right in the middle of what God is doing in these last days. My prayer is that you, too, will "catch the vision," and that we might be co-laborers in this end-time work for Almighty God.

What the Bridge Looks Like

It could be as simple as a fallen tree resting across a brook or as complicated as a bridge of cable and steel suspended high above a ravine. It may vary in size, length, and material, but its mission never changes. The function of a bridge is to link one side to the other. Its task is to create a path where there once was no way.

When the time came to construct a bridge across the Niagara River, the builders studied the problem and then devised a plan. Because of Niagara's swift current, the standard method of stringing the bridge cables by boat was impossible. Instead, a young boy was asked to fly a kite from one bank over to the other side. There, a friend caught the kite string and tied it to a nearby tree. Once that task was accomplished, a succession of heavier cords were pulled across the river until the all important steel support cable was secured on both sides of the "uncrossable" body of water.

No matter how insurmountable the difficulty, man has always been able to cross the uncrossable!

Yet, when it comes to spanning the empty space of the human heart, man consistently falls short. No man by himself has been capable of repairing the spiritual breach caused by Adam's sin.

But God has a plan, a way to bridge the gulf of sin. Let me tell you a story about this spiritual bridge that can span the chasm of sin.

The Chasm of Sin

When Adam sinned in the Garden of Eden, man's access to God was severed. Sinful man could not come into the presence of a holy God. You may be familiar with Michelangelo's painting in the Sistine Chapel portraying man as striving to reach out to the outstretched hand of God. Try though he might, man could not touch God's hand.

The gulf was too great.

Through the centuries, man could not fill that gulf caused by sin with animal sacrifices or pious deeds. All the blood of all the lambs ever born could not erase man's awful guilt from sin.

But God had a loving plan.

Before there was ever a need, God had a solution. Jesus, the Son of God, would become the lamb slain before the foundation of the world.

Jesus took the wood of His own cross and fashioned a bridge to span the gulf of sin!

He built an eternal bridge; and on the day of Pentecost, over 6,000 crossed that holy bridge and became children of God! The rupture of Satan's kingdom was so severe that at one point his followers cried out in dismay, **"...These that have turned the world upside down are come hither also" (Acts 17:6).**

Satan had to do something to destroy the bridge, so he began undermining the foundation of the Word of God in people's lives through religious tradition. Over the centuries, he has stolen so many planks from the bridge of God that multiplied thousands of sighing, dying, crying people can no longer get across. The breach

16

is too great. The day has come for us to start pointing our finger in the devil's face and command him to stop destroying the bridge.

Though these hurting people have been pushed down, beaten up, and left for dead with no one who seems to care, there is a remnant of people in our generation who are being called by God to rebuild the bridge. They will be the repairers of the breach, the restorers of the dwelling paths (Isaiah 58:12).

God is looking for a people who want to mend the torn and tattered lives, who want to heal the splintered and shattered marriages. He is looking for a people who want to reach out a loving hand to the homeless, the hurting, the hungry, and the desperate. God is looking for a people to tenderly touch the depraved, the diseased, and the dying.

It is time we stopped playing church and started being the church!

It is time we started repairing the breach, restoring our dwelling paths!

I have had it with the devil coming in whatever guise he chooses to steal the authority and the life from the Body of Christ. The devil has no answers – only Jesus has the answer for this wretched world.

You may think there are other answers to the world's problems, such as better government or more comprehensive food distribution programs. You may believe that things would get better if the government took better care of the poor.

Well, I happen to believe the poor are not the government's responsibility – they are ours! And the answer Jesus has for the world includes helping the poor, feeding the hungry, and clothing the naked.

> **"The Spirit of the Lord is upon me, because he
> hath anointed me to preach the gospel to the poor;
> he hath sent me to heal the brokenhearted, to preach
> deliverance to the captives, and recovering of sight to**

the blind, to set at liberty them that are bruised, To preach the acceptable year of the Lord."

Luke 4:18-19

What was the purpose of that anointing?

Was it to build a larger ministry mailing list or to construct the biggest church in town? Was it to have our names plastered all over Christian magazines so that when we walk down the street everybody knows us?

No! No! No!

Jesus said His anointing was for healing, for deliverance, to set at liberty those who are bruised!

Preacher, if you want to fill up your church, get your attention off the "church growth methods" of the world and challenge your people to street ministry. Open a shelter for the homeless. Minister to your neighbors who are on crack.

The poor, the brokenhearted, and the sick are waiting to hear the gospel!

The remnant church is not going to be a church satisfied with newly padded pews, crystal chandeliers, megamedia programs, and preachers who are so slick-haired and shiny-shoed that the downcast of this world are afraid to reach out a trembling and weakened hand to the kingdom of God for help.

God is looking for a church that will reach out one hand to the gutter and the other hand into glory and pull the two together!

It is time to start repairing the breach between heaven and the gutter!

The Gap Closes

One man at a shelter for the homeless in our city first heard about World Harvest Church (where I pastor) standing outside a store that sold televisions. In the window, there were several televisions playing on different channels. By "divine coincidence," one of the televisions "just happened" to be tuned to a Christian station.

This homeless man saw one of our services through the store window; and he declared in his heart, "God, I want to get there."

He then took a step of faith and rode one of our outreach ministry buses from the shelter where he was staying to church service. When he first came, he was wearing ragged clothes and walking on worn shoes. But the Spirit of God was there to span the chasm, to close the breach, and this precious man gave his life to Christ that day! Within a short time, this man was off the streets, out of the shelter, had a home and a job, was well dressed, and became an usher in our church!

God wants to use each one of us to bridge the gap between the gutter and heaven.

A young woman with a $250-a-day crack cocaine habit saw our television program. She saw how nice everyone looked at our church, and she knew she did not have pretty clothes to wear. But she didn't let that stop her. "I don't have the right clothes to wear, but I am going to go to that church."

She was desperate.

Her family was destroyed, and her body had been ravaged by crack.

This searching lady called a taxi to get to church and barely had enough money to pay for the fare. She took the journey out of the gutter to attend a World Harvest Church service, believing God could do something for her. Attired in a tank top and a pair of old cut-off blue jeans with holes in them, she came forward for prayer when I gave the altar call. Her body was emaciated; her eyes sunk back into her head.

I will never forget how she looked that day as she stood in front of me trembling. Standing on the promises of God, I reached one hand into the gutter and the other into glory and declared, "In the name of Jesus, you demon spirit of crack cocaine, come out of this precious woman!"

She was instantly set free!

These two simple stories are representative of the multiplied millions of desperate, searching people who are waiting for someone to rebuild the bridge to get them across into the hands of Jesus.

This bridge was designed for the down and out *and* the up and out – those who have "made it" financially and socially in our society but still do not know God. They, too, need the bridge so they can come into God's kingdom, bringing the offerings of their time, talent, and treasure with them. The day is coming when their trembling hands will reach out for a hand that is bigger than theirs. They need Jesus, too.

Rebuild and Keep the Bridge

It is time to restore Bible basics and rebuild the bridge. Not only are we going to rebuild it, we are going to keep it.

> **"...If a man keep my saying, he shall never see death."**
>
> **John 8:51**

The word "keep" is from the Greek word "tereo," which means to place in a position of absolute protection, to chaperone as one would protect his virgin daughters.

God wants to protect His Word and His people!

We possess precious virgin truths that the devil and his bunch of religious heretics have ripped from the bridge – planks of truth that must be restored to secure God's blessings for a hurting humanity. It is time we declared, "Devil, not only are you going to leave the bridge alone, but you are going to replace all the planks of truth in God's bridge of grace that you have stolen."

It is time to repair the breach, to restore it once and for all!

Yours for the harvest,
Rod Parsley, Pastor
World Harvest Church
Columbus, Ohio

PLANK ONE

**Restoring Holiness
to the Body of Christ**

PLANK ONE

Restoring Holiness
to the Body of Christ

"The Pet Rattler"

The Memphis Commercial Appeal carried a news dispatch which told of a man across the river in Arkansas who had a pet rattlesnake. The man found the snake as a baby snake. He took it and fed it and made quite a pet of it. The reptile would come when he whistled. It would eat from his fingers. It would coil around his arm and let him stroke its head with the palm of his hand or with the tips of his fingers.

One day he took it to town to exhibit it among his friends. They marveled at its gentleness – marveled at the way it coiled itself with apparent gentleness around his arm – marveled how it would come when he whistled – marveled that it would eat from his hand.

He went back home with his pet. When he got home, suddenly, with only the slightest provocation, the reptile became angry. Quicker than a zigzag lightning flashes from the bosom of a dark cloud, that pet rattler buried its fangs in the man's arm.

In a few hours, the man was dead.

In one quick instant, with poisonous fangs, the serpent had written his death in his own blood! Two nights after that, the man who should have been sitting with his family in their humble but happy home was sleeping in the mud of an Arkansas grave.

With such dread cometh such an hour to every man and woman who makes a pet of sin.

So cometh such a horror and death to every man who refuses when God calls.

An hour of kindred terror awaits the man or the woman who guards not when God stretches out His hand. A day of dreaded despair like that man met when he pulled the pet snake's fangs from his arm and hurled it to the ground, is waiting for all those who set at naught God's counsel and will have none of His reproof.

> "Be not deceived; God is not mocked."
> Turn you at God's reproof! Turn now!
> There's danger and death in delay.
> Let go that sin!
> Drop it – now!

— Robert G. Lee in
Whirlwinds of God[1]

Free From the Slavery of Sin

"Again the word of the Lord came unto me, saying, Son of man, speak to the children of thy people, and say unto them, When I bring the sword upon a land, if the people of the land take a man of their coasts, and set him for their watchman: If when he seeth the sword come upon the land, he blow the trumpet, and warn the people; Then whosoever heareth the sound of the trumpet, and taketh not warning; if the sword come, and take him away, his blood shall be upon his own head.

"So thou, O son of man, I have set thee a watchman unto the house of Israel; therefore thou shalt hear the word at my mouth, and warn them from me. When I say unto the wicked, O wicked man, thou shalt surely die; if thou dost not speak to warn the wicked from his way, that wicked man shall die in his iniquity; but his blood will I require at thine hand. Nevertheless, if thou warn the wicked of his way to turn from it; if he do not turn from his way, he shall die in his iniquity; but thou hast delivered thy soul."

Ezekiel 33:1-4, 7-9

Gangland violence and drive-by shootings frequent the front pages of our daily papers. Homicide incidents have escalated to an all-time high. An insidious plague ravages our global populace in the form of the destructive medical condition called AIDS. Some sources tell us over fifty percent of all marriages crash land into revolving door divorce courts, leaving innocent children left to pick up the shattered pieces of their tiny lives.

Big money cocaine cartels prosper. Payoffs become part of the political process. Sex scandals permeate every sphere of our society.

25

We continue to live in the silent screams of fear, and to hurt from the blank stare on the faces of the homeless who moan under the hollowness of an empty stomach and the despair of poverty.

We continue to clamor for war to solve our moral problems, and fail to stem the plague of AIDS. We live in the cruelty of deceit and the snobbery of pride.

Murder invades every neighborhood, and families are ravaged by the helplessness of divorce. Abortionists continue to kill children to line their silk pockets with dollars. The gnawing of cancer, the limp of one who is lame, and the cold ache of arthritis persist in crippling the living.

In my spirit, I hear the cry of a little girl who sobs quietly in her bed at night, tears staining her pillow as she gently nurses the black-and-blue bruise on her precious cheek. Daddy came home with too much to drink and struck that little girl, sending her to bed, a cheerless cheerleader.

In the next house lies a lonely little leaguer whose daddy is too busy climbing the corporate ladder to be his full-time father.

In another room is a sweet wife who sits in fear and trembling from the abuse of her husband, driven to drink because of unemployment. He cannot perform the work he has been trained to do and cannot pay his bills – a rage burns within his soul. This rage he feels over his depressing circumstances releases in violence upon his wife.

Families continue to be ravaged, aimlessly led by an immoral media, battered in every possible way through their existence on this planet. Fear of the past, the present, and the future permeates our culture. Only hospitals and ambulance sirens, county jails and federal penitentiaries seem to flourish, along with slander, lying, cheating, and stealing.

We are seeing the insane effects of sin!

We are experiencing a taste of the reality and the certainty of an eternal hell.

But no one wants to talk about it.

So sexual perversion, homosexuality, and incest increase.

The chains of addiction to alcohol and drugs continue.

Funeral homes and morgues prosper.

Rape, demon possession, and spiritual slavery live in the blackness of our midnight. A pagan religious tradition binds the spirits, minds, and bodies of men in the chains of their own philosophic ideas and lack of faith in anything but themselves.

In an atmosphere of sin, we endure slavery and prejudice, and maintain our silence even in the atrocities of death. The hideousness of Hitler's holocaust and Hussein's invasion of Kuwait are tolerated along with suicide, abortion, and teenaged pregnancy.

The world offers empty answers in the occult and astrology. Welcome to the New Age of deceit!

The world writhes in the pains of birth as the end-time clock ticks closer and closer to its expiration. Society winces at the sight of repeated reports of cruel, heinous, criminal activity. In the midst of worldwide tumult, a hungry society searches desperately for answers.

Meanwhile, the majority of the church lies in wreckage and ruin, completely powerless – unable to offer any semblance of consolation or help to a struggling world.

But there is help – and it is in God's Word!

> **"...and thou shalt be called, The repairer of the breach, The restorer of paths to dwell in."**
>
> **Isaiah 58:12**

Take Back What Satan Has Stolen!

There is an enormous breach, a chasm between God and His creation, man. But across that vast expanse stretches a bridge, a gospel bridge constructed by Jesus Christ Himself, paved and planked with gospel truths: salvation, healing, deliverance, and many more.

There has been an intruder, a thief who has stolen, broken, and dismantled the very planks constructed for our safety.

That thief is Satan.

I am angry at what the devil has done, and I want to expose it and repair it through the grace God has already given to us!

The devil and his sinister hordes have raped the gospel of its power. That power has dissipated into the misty haze of New Age crystal conventions and eastern mysticism. The power of the gospel message has been seduced out of the hands of today's Christians by humanist theologians who feel the virgin birth is nothing more than an ancient relic of historic folklore, and that the resurrection is only a figurative symbolism used to illustrate a dramatic science fiction tale of good guys defeating the bad ones.

It is time to declare to the devil, "That's enough."

It is time to stop compromise and friendly coexistence with sin.

It is time for confrontation, not accommodation!

It is time to meet the devil head to head, to tell him to go home and get his hammer and nails, and then command him to nail back in place every plank he has stolen.

In this chapter, you will see how Satan and his cohorts have succeeded in stealing the plank of holiness from the gospel bridge through the corrosive and corruptive nature of sin. It is time we put the plank of holiness back into the teachings of the church.

Shattered Mirrors, Broken Lives

I was called to an emergency at the house next door to my parent's home. The house had been ravaged – windows had been broken, furniture overturned, drawers pulled out, mirrors broken, beds turned upside down, and clothing and other things were thrown out in the middle of the floor.

Later, I learned that a fifteen-year-old boy high on crack cocaine had kicked in a window and spent several days living in this home.

When the police arrived at the scene, the boy ran from the home, across a field, and jumped into a filthy, dirty, putrid swamp filled with stagnant water with green algae floating all over the top.

Yet, the boy deliberately dove into that swamp! As the police pulled him out, he began to scream and kick, cursing like I have never heard before. Words of profanity I did not even know existed began a deluge out of that fifteen-year-old's mouth. His words were far dirtier than the swamp water.

Shocked and amazed by the scene, I asked the police officer, a good friend of mine, "How does a person end up in this pathetic condition in just fifteen short years on this planet?"

He looked me in the eye and told me what I already knew: "Pastor Parsley, he didn't get that way overnight."

When they placed the young boy in the police cruiser, he beat his head against the inside of that vehicle until blood was running down his face. He screamed and kicked like a wild man. They cuffed his hands in front of him; yet, he still managed to raise them over his back and get them behind him, cutting his arms in several places. His hands were bleeding.

While the police were trying to calm the boy down, a report came over the police cruiser's radio system that there had been an accident. Another cruiser which had been called by the dispatcher to that burglary was driving at a high rate of speed to get to the scene where that fifteen-year-old was causing such a disturbance.

As the cruiser sped down the highway, there was a car in front of them full of teenagers and their driving instructor. The student driver saw the lights behind him and panicked, trying to pull out of the way. The young driver thought the police were going to the right, but they swerved back to the left; and that police cruiser crashed into the side of that driver's education car.

Three people died.

The newly captured boy had no idea any of this had happened. Instead, he was only concerned for his own welfare. He looked into the eyes of the arresting police officer and asked, "Why don't you just go ahead and release me? I am a juvenile, and you know they'll let me go anyway."

The policeman ignored the boy's request and took him to juvenile hall. In less than three hours, the youngster was released on his own recognizance.

This nagging thought stirred in my heart after this incident: A fifteen-year-old boy thought he was out for a joy ride and would get away with it. If only someone could have taught him the timeless biblical principle that **"The wages of sin is death" (Romans 6:23).**

The youngster had no earthly idea that three people would be ushered into eternity – two of them sixteen-year-olds who would never see their seventeenth birthday, as a result of his rebellion.

What was the root cause of this destruction?

Sin – a highly infectious, communicable disease!

The World's Swamp of Sin

Imagine, that young boy tried to escape from the police by diving into a putrid swamp. As filthy and disease-infected as that green water was, the police still had to drag that boy, kicking and screaming, from the horrid place.

America today is wallowing in a swamp of perversion and filth; yet, it seems our people are so adjusted to the green, filthy water that it will take caring and determined preachers to literally pull these lost souls from the mire of their lives, to tell them there is a way to break the devil's power so that they can begin to live again as free men and women – the way God originally intended.

We live in a wretched world, deep in moral decline. We are riding on a bobsled headed straight for hell; yet, no one wants to talk about sin – so we unwittingly continue to bathe in slimy swamp water.

Without any apparent hope, broken, the jagged edges tear at relationships. Backbiting, insensitivity, and whispering divide even the best of friends. Unfaithfulness mangles marriages, bringing tears to eyes which sadly reflect the pain in our hearts and the wounds in our souls.

But no one wants to talk about it.

We pretend sin does not exist.

We stick our heads into the philosophic sand of deception and seek the earthly security that declares: "I've laid my treasure up in barns, I've gathered in my crop. My soul is made fat. When I get too much, I'll tear down my small barns, and I'll build larger barns."

It is time to hear the ringing, resounding words of our Heavenly Father, who declares a different message than the materialism so exalted in our swamp-water society:

> **"Thou fool, this night thy soul shall be required of thee: then whose shall those things be, which thou hast provided?"**
>
> **Luke 12:20**

If we do not take care of this sin-sick disease currently plaguing the life of humanity, we are bound for hell as fast as the unlocked wheels of time will carry us.

Satan has stolen the plank of holiness from our bridge – and a huge chasm of sin keeps us from our Creator!

Sin Separates

Sin is everything cruel, painful, fierce, and ravaging. It is every plague, curse, and blight known to the human family. To satisfy its ceaseless cravings, men will sell their souls; and many will spend eternity in hell trying to fill the void of its gnawing hunger.

Sin produces a separation between the Creator and His creation; it is the chasm between God and man.

But no one wants to talk about it.

> **"Furthermore then we beseech you, brethren, and exhort you by the Lord Jesus, that as ye have received of us how ye ought to walk and to please God, so ye would abound more and more."**
>
> **1 Thessalonians 4:1**

31

Do you see the connection between obeying God, pleasing Him – and abounding in this life? If Christians are to clean up this swamp we now call "earth," if we are to abound in God's goodness, we must eradicate sin in our lives.

There are only two types of people who walk the face of the earth today – the saved and the damned.

I pray the Holy Ghost will put the on-fire Christians on one side of a divine line and breathe His breath on them until they become hotter, and that He will lead the cold sinners on the other side to recognize sin, repent, and cross over to the side of the righteous! (God is **"not willing that any should perish, but that all should come to repentance" 2 Peter 3:9.**)

The differences need to be made clear between those who are saved and those who are damned! Put sin on one side of the divine line and righteousness on the other, health on one side and sickness on the other.

The divine dividing line is clearly drawn in **John 10:10: "The thief cometh not, but for to steal, and to kill, and to destroy: I am come that they might have life, and that they might have it more abundantly."**

Destruction or life – that is the choice.

If you warn the wicked man of his wicked deeds and he heeds your warning, he lives!

If you warn the wicked man of his wicked deeds and he rejects your warning, he will die.

The Bible plainly declares these penetrating words: **"...the soul that sinneth, it shall die" (Ezekiel 18:4).**

This is a life-changing message. I am not writing this book to lightly tickle your flesh and barely touch your spirit. I hope, by the grace and the help of the Spirit of the living God, to unveil and expose to you the most cruel and diabolical scheme, the most penetrating, devastating disease known to the human family.

When you see sin clearly, I believe you will zero the Word of God in on it, driving the enemy out of your life so that he no longer holds you captive in any area.

We are not going to ignore sin any longer!

We are not going to pretend sin does not exist! Too many people have already slipped through this hole in the bridge on their way to hell!

"For the wages of sin is death; but the gift of God is eternal life through Jesus Christ our Lord."
Romans 6:23

That is the choice – "eternal life" or "eternal damnation." The Word promises life of a superior quality – the life of the Creator lived through and expressed by His creation.

The Bible promises, **"And ye shall know the truth, and the truth** [regardless of how it cuts you] **shall make you free" (John 8:32).** The Word of God is sharper than any two-edged sword (Hebrews 4:12): It cuts going in; and it heals coming out.

"For the wages of sin is death."
Romans 6:23

God Intended Mercy and Goodness

Creation was not born in sin and iniquity. When God created the heavens and the earth, He called it good (Genesis 1:10). He planted a tree in the midst of the Garden of Eden, called the tree of the knowledge of good and evil (Genesis 2:9). He formed a man from the dust of the ground, breathed into his nostrils the breath of life, and man became a living soul (Genesis 2:7). Adam and Eve walked with God in the blessedness of Eden, until suddenly the serpent appeared and beguiled them.

God did not create the earth in a condition of sin and wretchedness.

But, with one exposure of the yielded human spirit to the corruption of Satan, suddenly the bloodstream of every living, breathing human born of a woman was infused and inundated with the curse of sin.

33

I know any teaching on sin is not popular. But we cannot ignore that sin exists; and when it enters our lives, it will affect us, no matter how we try to cover it up.

Adam and Eve stood in the Garden of Eden and ate of the tree of the knowledge of good and evil. Instead of receiving the false promises of the serpent, they received "the knowledge" of every putrid and sickening disease, every infirmity and wickedness. They became clothed in the filthy rags of righteousness.

Adam saw he was naked; and, at the same time, he gained a keen awareness of every good and every perfect gift whose blessings now lay just an inch away from his outstretched, sin-infected hand.

A chasm had been created by sin, a separation over which he could not pass. He found himself inundated, infused, and deluged with the problems of his once perfect world. His very bloodstream now flowed with sin, iniquity, and perversion.

From Eden to Calvary's Tree

Sin was introduced into the world when one man reached for a piece of fruit under a tree. The cure for sin was birthed by another man who hung on a tree for you and me.

> **"For as by one man's disobedience many were made sinners, so by the obedience of one shall many be made righteous."**
>
> **Romans 5:19**

Sin exists in our world, and it is time we start talking about it, and its dreadful consequences. My heart longs to hear from our pulpits some old-fashioned, Holy Ghost messages on the not-so-popular subject of hell. I long to hear life-changing sermons about the prospects of spending an eternity in a place where the worm dieth not, the fire is not quenched, where men gnaw their tongues for pain, and where the smoke of their torment ascends forever (Mark 9:43-44).

I want someone to tell America the truth!

There is a heaven to gain and a hell to shun!

The truth may not be popular, but it is real; and I am going to shout it to America – **"The soul that sinneth, it shall die" (Ezekiel 18:4).**

Thank God, through the provision of Calvary, you and I no longer have to be bondslaves to sin. We can be free, infused with an eternal blood transfusion from Golgotha's hillside.

At this point, you may have the same question that is resounding in the soul and mind of every member of the human family on this earth today: "What you say is probably true, but how do I get from where I am (a sinner) to where I need to be (saved)?

Let me answer that question with a simple story.

My Uncle Willie was an alcoholic for thirty-five years, until he decided that he was thoroughly disgusted with the sickness, nausea, and unpredictable behavior that accompany alcoholism. He confessed his sins, repented, and received a total deliverance from alcohol through the blood of Jesus. For thirty-five years, Uncle Willie had asked, "How can I be free?"

But only after he tried all the answers of the world did he finally say, "Okay Jesus, I have tried everything the world has to offer, with no success. Now, I am giving my life to You."

God can transform the world's swamps into life-giving oceans of divine grace!

When I write about sin, please understand I am not just writing to the prostitute and the drunkard. I pray that the Spirit of God is also speaking to you.

If you think you are free from the chains of sin, you are wrong!

Lurking somewhere in your mind or somewhere in your body are the effects of the curse of sin. But as you examine the sinful areas in your life and offer them up to God, He will cleanse your heart and give you His divine freedom.

"If we confess our sins, he is faithful and just to forgive us our sins, and to cleanse us from all unrighteousness."

1 John 1:9

Obedience Is the Key

How do you get from where you currently are to where you need to be?

Obedience to the will of God.

I do not mean obedience to your will, or the will of your neighborhood pastor, or to the will of your denomination. You get where you need to be through obedience to the will of God!

You do not have to conform to the measuring stick or the opinions of others; let the Word of God be your only check and balance. Let it be the lone standard whereby you measure yourself. The Word of the Almighty is the just balance and the weight of delight.

To understand how God requires our obedience, consider the story of Naaman the leper in 2 Kings 5. Naaman was an affluent and powerful man, captain of the host, yet his skin was marred by leprosy. He went to inquire of the prophet Elisha to see if he could be delivered from his terminal disease.

The prophet did not even come to the door; instead, he sent a messenger to speak to Naaman. Elisha's instructions through the messenger were clear. Naaman was told,

"Go and wash in Jordan seven times, and thy flesh shall come again to thee, and thou shalt be clean."

2 Kings 5:10

At first, Naaman was highly insulted that he had been told, through a messenger, to go soak himself in the muddy Jordan River. He even complained that he had wasted his time taking the journey to Israel, especially because there were clearer waters in Damascus (2 Kings 5:12).

Finally, when Naaman's humble servant reminded him that these were the instructions of God's prophet, Naaman obeyed God's Word; and upon dipping in the Jordan River the seventh time, he came out of the water with **"...the flesh of a little child, and he was clean" (2 Kings 5:14).**

Does Naaman's story sound a bit like the Christians of today?

"Lord, we don't do it that way at our church," we cry. "Could You please change Your instructions to line up with our doctrine?"

To cleanse our world of the spiritual leprosy that has permeated every aspect of our society, all we need to do is to become obedient to the will of God!

Knowing God's Will

To be obedient, you must first know His will before you can follow it. Today, the Body of Christ is not being taught the entire will of God; we are only given those things that are pleasant to hear.

For example, we hear from our preachers that it is God's will for us to prosper.

> **"Beloved, I wish above all things that thou mayest prosper and be in health, even as thy soul prospereth."**
>
> **3 John 2**

Yes, that scripture is true – it *is* the will of God to prosper us in every area of our lives. It *is* the will of God for us to walk in divine health.

But those are not the spiritual truths which will set you free from the icy tentacles of sin, which will keep you from being brought down into despair and the damnation of your soul when life is over.

Sanctification First

The will of God that will set you free is sanctification – being set apart. God said to Abraham, **"Come out from among them, and be ye separate…" (2 Corinthians 6:17).**

But today we are too busy to obey.

Some Christians sanctify and set apart church buildings and mission programs; they dedicate and sanctify buses and vans, even the preacher's car. They anoint everything with oil, including the pews.

God desires to sanctify more than a temple made with human hands. It is the three-part being called man whom God wants to separate unto Himself.

Just as God wants to separate the alcoholic's mouth from the bottle of booze, He wants to separate every part of your life from the bondages and the tentacles of corruptive sin.

Sanctification frees your body from the torment and after-effects of sin – disease – it closes the gap that sin opens on your bridge to God.

Remember, both those who are not born again and those who are born again have a problem with sin; sometimes we fail to admit this. What kind of philosophical madness we Christians practice! If a man strikes his wife before he is born again, we call it a sin. If he strikes her after he is born again, we announce it as a problem and send him to counseling.

Sin is something we all have in common!

Whether you are black or white, have straight, strawberry blonde hair or curly, black hair, whether you are rich or poor, tall or short, from uptown or downtown, a Democrat or a Republican – sin is sin!

The one thing we all have in common that no one wants to talk about is sin. It is time to expose sin and force it out of our lives by the power of the Holy Ghost.

Sanctification is the impartation of divine grace whereby we are made holy. We have huge crowds of worldlings on their way to hell in the "love boat" while so-called Christians are lulled into a deep sleep on the "dove boat." Yet, Christian and non-Christian passengers both look and act the same – full of envy, pride, deceitfulness, jealousy, and backbiting.

What kind of sanctification is it when we get saved and stop smoking but continue backbiting? When we renounce drugs and secretly read pornography? We need to get rid of backbiting, destroy pride, and let our tongues become sanctified and holy unto God.

It is time to warn the church.

Call a solemn assembly.

> **"Blow ye the trumpet in Zion, and sound an alarm in my holy mountain: let all the inhabitants of the land tremble: for the day of the Lord cometh, for it is nigh at hand."**
>
> **Joel 2:1**

Some people, after they are born again, refuse to darken the door of a movie theater – and God bless them; that is good. But what do they do next? They go to their local video store and bring R-rated filth into their own homes!

It is time to drive the devil completely out of our camp and begin to let the Holy Ghost flood our lives with cleansing waters.

To follow the will of God, we must follow His entire will – not just the parts we enjoy, such as the messages on healing and prosperity. We must be completely sanctified!

When I write about holiness, I am not writing about wearing somber, long-sleeved outfits and walking around without a trace of a smile. I am not interested in the length or color of your hair, or whether you have buttons or zippers on your newest jacket.

But, I know it is vital for you to experience real sanctification – where His divine grace cleanses you and makes you holy.

No Self-Sanctification

Sanctification is not something you can do for yourself. Try hard as you might, you do not have the power by yourself to change the inner man.

Let me illustrate.

You can try to change the sinful flesh of a prostitute by dressing her in a $5,000 mink stole, sitting her in a $50,000 luxury car, dabbing $200-an-ounce perfume behind her ear lobes, and affixing a $20,000 diamond bracelet on her wrist. You can put every kind of precious jewel on her body and anoint her with the sweet fragrances of a thousand nations. Yet, when she drives down the road, underneath it all she is still, unfortunately, nothing but sinful flesh on her way to hell.

We cannot sanctify ourselves.

We need to passionately cry out," God, sanctify me wholly."

> **"And the very God of peace sanctify you wholly;
> and I pray God your whole spirit and soul and body
> be preserved blameless unto the coming of our Lord
> Jesus Christ."**
>
> **1 Thessalonians 5:23**

We need to cry, "God, do for me what I cannot do! Deliver me from this body of death."

You cannot sanctify yourself. Sanctification only happens by yielding your human spirit to the blessed Holy Ghost of God within you. He will guide you and direct you into all truth and free you from your self-willed, worldly indulgences.

Salvation does not dismiss sin's power from the earth, but it will give you personally the power to resist every temptation and stop the corrosive effects of sin in your own life. Through the Holy Ghost, you can walk in victory over every temptation.

Rise Above Circumstances

Sanctification is the possibility of living beyond the grasp of your adversary so that you do not dwell on the magnitude of your current circumstances, but instead trust in the mighty power of your God to resolve every area of your life! Your hope is in God Almighty, and He can help you rise above the scope of human limitations as you dwell on His Word.

> **"...he that is begotten of God keepeth himself, and that wicked one toucheth him not."**
>
> **1 John 5:18**

Imagine – the devil cannot touch you because you are being protected and kept by God!

When God sanctifies you, that will happen.

Even Jesus went through a sanctification process. Jesus said, in His high priestly prayer,

> **"And for their sakes I sanctify myself, that they also might be sanctified through the truth."**
>
> **John 17:19**

Jesus was sanctified unto the Father. He was saying, "The works I do are not My own; they are the works of Him that sent Me. The words that I speak, they are not My own; they are the words of Him that sent Me. The will that I accomplish is not My own; I come to do the will of Him who sent Me." (John 17).

Jesus was sanctified through the Father.

> **"Believest thou not that I am in the Father, and the Father in me? the words that I speak unto you I speak not of myself: but the Father that dwelleth in me, he doeth the works."**
>
> **John 14:10**

We come to the Father through Jesus.

"I am the way, the truth, and the life: no man cometh unto the Father, but by me."

John 14:6

And through the Father, like Jesus, we are sanctified to become victorious over all of our circumstances and adversities.

"He that believeth on me, the works that I do shall he do also; and greater works than these shall he do; because I go unto my Father."

John 14:12

Oh, for Christians who will totally give themselves completely to God.

Oh, for a church who will shake off the tentacles of worldliness and live where the evil one touches them not.

I long for a time when the Lord stands at the edge of our Christian lives and declares, "They are mine; they are bought with a price. Devil, do not touch them."

Don't you long to be wholly God's?

When you are, no matter how devastating or hopeless your current circumstances might seem to be, He will give you the strength to rise above them in peace and trust Him, living each day beyond the grasp of your adversary.

When Jesus told the Jews, **"...Before Abraham was, I am"** (John 8:58), they wanted to stone and kill Him. But the Bible tells us that Jesus **"went out of the temple, going through the midst of them, and so passed by" (John 8:59).** Jesus was not affected by the crowd! By the time they had picked up their stones, He had calmly walked through the crisis to perform His next miracle.

When the Israelites were being rescued by God from their seemingly impossible circumstances and were confronted with the Egyptians behind them and the Red Sea in front of them, **"By faith they passed through the Red Sea as by dry land..." (Hebrews 11:29).**

When Shadrach, Meshach, and Abednego were thrown into a furnace seven times hotter than normal – a fire so hot it killed the men putting God's servants into it – they walked **"...in the midst of the fire, and they have no hurt; and the form of the fourth is like the Son of God" (Daniel 3:25).**

Do you see it? God walked through that fire with them! God personally protected Shadrach, Meshach, and Abednego and "kept" them safe from the flames and the heat of their circumstances!

When you are sanctified into the presence of God, you can be thrown into the fiery furnace of life and come out the other end not smelling like smoke; you can pass through the fire and it will not burn you; you can be struck by a flood but you will not drown.

Why?

Because you have been sanctified, protected, and kept safely by God, called to a holy, higher purpose. That is the will of God for your life!

Repentance, Not Apology

It is the will of God for you to abstain from fornication and licentiousness and all sin. One of the biggest lies ever known to man is the popular statement: "The devil made me do it." You are born again and Spirit-filled – God has given you the strength to resist sin; there are no excuses – no one to blame.

Where there is an excuse, there is no repentance.

True repentance is not apology. "I am sorry" is not repentance. Repentance is, "By the grace of Almighty God, I will never set my sails in the direction of that sin again. Through the power of the Holy Ghost, I am turning my back on the devil forever. Lord, I repent of sin in my life."

Do you know what will bless your church and your family – when you fall down prostrate before God and plead, "God, sanctify my mind, sanctify my body, sanctify my house."

Peter wrote about the results of such repentance:

"Repent ye therefore, and be converted, that
your sins may be blotted out, when the times of re-
freshing shall come from the presence of the Lord."

Acts 3:19

True repentance will bring refreshing, cleansing waves from the throne of God – and your sins will be forever blotted out!

You cannot repent or be sanctified by yourself. You have tried; you cannot do it. But there is one who can make your life off-limits to the devil, taking you totally beyond the adversary's power. Let the Holy Ghost help you understand that your battle is not at the Red Sea or the fiery furnace – those are just the current circumstances. Your real battle takes place in the spirit world – where God has given you the power to pull down every earthly stronghold!

God is not looking for a church that sends its spiritual arsenal into the heavenlies. God is looking for a church that will turn its gun turrets on the ravages of sin in the lives of its people, driving out the demonic intruders who have stolen the spiritual power and anointing from the church.

It is time to abandon the pathetic gospel of self-preservation where we perform plastic surgery on our spiritual lives – pluck out this problem, paint this one up a bit, powder that one so it does not stink as much, puff up this part of your ego.

The philosophies of self-help and self-preservation have invaded and diluted our spiritual lives!

Go into any Christian bookstore and browse through the catalogs; try to find one book on the subject of sin, repentance, and sanctification. You will find books stacked to the ceiling on spiritual self-preservation. You will find more books on Christian aerobics than you will on the subject of sin.

Church, the reality today is that you will find more people at prosperity seminars than you will find at the altar crying out to God to sanctify them from this world.

Some of you may think, "That's a negative confession about the condition of the church."

No, it is not negative – it is simply the truth!

The real negative force is when we tell our people to mask over their sin by encouraging them to go to a prosperity seminar, and then watch as a wicked divorce ravages their home and leaves the children without a mommy or a daddy.

Now, do not misunderstand me here. The prosperity preachers are bringing to the Body of Christ a needed portion of the gospel. But our desire for any material prosperity must be balanced against a deep hunger for the anointing of Almighty God in our lives.

My prayer, my life's quest, is a cry deep within my soul: "God, give us a church and a people full of the anointing, cleansed from all that is unholy."

I hate sin, and I hate what it does to man.

That is not a negative message.

Is it negative to live right?

To be free from the ravages of sin?

I declare to you that it is not hard to live right and be free if you are sanctified in Jesus Christ; through His power, you will not find yourself lusting after the sins of the flesh.

I know this from experience. I waited seven years for my wife; Dr. Lester Sumrall called it my "tribulation period." After seven years, I made it through the tribulation period and on into heaven. I love my wife so much that I have prayed for God to sanctify my eyes so that every other woman on the face of this earth pales in insignificance next to the wonderful beauty God has placed in my life.

Is it hard to live right?

Only if you wallow in the swamp of sin.

The Bible says **"...the way of transgressors is hard" (Proverbs 13:15).**

Jesus said, **"For my yoke is easy, and my burden is light" (Matthew 11:30).**

You can be free by His blood to live without struggle, without defeat, without stress and strife. You can do it because **"...greater is he that is in you, than he that is in the world" (1 John 4:4).**

Savor the Moments

God wants you to enjoy and savor every moment of your life and to overcome life's little problems (ALL of your problems are little – easy to resolve – to God).

When our daughter, Ashton, was little, I would wake up as she ran into our bedroom and jumped up on my chest, questioning, "Daddy, are you awake?" I would feel a little finger poke me in the eye. Sometimes I would already be awake, but I would pretend I was still asleep. Now maybe some would view a finger in the eye as a problem; but to me, those moments of sudden shock are as treasured as silver or gold.

Ask God to allow you to savor the moments of your life. Sanctification and the resulting peace are available only from the cross of Calvary, where God has a full supply of His riches waiting for you.

> **"And the very God of peace sanctify you wholly; and I pray God your whole spirit and soul and body be preserved blameless unto the coming of our Lord Jesus Christ."**
> **1 Thessalonians 5:23**

Do not let anyone tell you that you have to sin daily in thought, word, and deed; anyone who believes that needs to get saved. My Bible declares, **"...greater is he that is in you, than he that is in the world" (1 John 4:4).**

God is looking for a church so inundated and infused with the power of God that it points its finger under the devil's nose and says, "Get behind me, Satan. Greater is He that is in me than he that is in the world."

God is looking for a people who will resist every temptation and live in holiness, purity, and power before Him.

> **"For as many as are led by the Spirit of God,**
> **they are the sons of God."**
>
> **Romans 8:14**

They are led by the Spirit and have no desire to look like the world. Christian, stop seeing how close to the world you can get and still be saved. Rather, see how far away from the world you can get and still be on this planet!

Do not love the world or the things in the world; the world has nothing to offer.

> **"For all that is in the world, the lust of the flesh,**
> **and the lust of the eyes, and the pride of life, is not of**
> **the Father, but is of the world."**
>
> **1 John 2:16**

Do you know what the lust of the flesh is? It is when you want what God told you not to have.

Do you know what the lust of the eye is? It is when you take pleasure in seeing what you will not do.

An interesting article in our local newspaper contained a recap of a popular soap opera. In case you missed an episode, you could read about it in the paper! The article described in graphic detail the sordid, sin-filled lives of the cast of characters. You could read everything that had happened on the last program – 28 minutes and 50 seconds of who was having whose baby, who was leaving who, and why. It was 28 minutes and 50 seconds worth of devastating, debilitating tragedy.

Now, the devil tries to lie to you by saying, "Oh, it is just a television soap opera. Go ahead and watch it. After all, you are a strong enough Christian not to be influenced by that stuff."

Recognize the lie and renounce it!

There is no such thing as, "Oh, a little flesh never hurt anybody." Think about it. You would never let another man's wife have your baby, but you willingly watch it on television *and* take pleasure in the story.

To watch it is to take pleasure in it.

To permit it is to participate in it.

It is time to cut ourselves free from sin and be sanctified unto God. Let us return to a message of holiness and power in the church.

When John Wesley (founder of the Methodist church) was a young man, he asked his mother one day, "How do we know what forms of entertainment are all right for us to participate in?"

His mother told him, "Anything that impedes the tenderness of your conscience, weakens your reason, obscures your sense of God, or dulls your deep desire of spiritual things; anything which exalts the will of your soul and body over your spirit, that thing to you is sin."

We would all do well to heed the words of John Wesley's mother.

The Three Sanctifications

One of your main spiritual goals is to walk in His holy sanctification – purified, cleansed, and empowered to share the gospel!

The experience of sanctification in your life will ultimately cover three stages:

1. Positional Sanctification: This is accomplished when you are born again, when God separates you from this world. When you are born again of the Spirit of God, you are saved and your spirit is sanctified.

There is instilled in you a spirit which will sustain all your infirmity.

"The spirit of a man will sustain his infirmity…"
Proverbs 18:14

This sustaining spirit will help you to recognize and resist temptation. When temptation flirts with you, your mind might say, "I want to do this"; but if you will listen to your spirit, you will hear, "Don't have anything to do with that temptation. Your only desire is for God. You need to keep focused on Him and remain hungry for more of God."

When you want more of Him as much as you want to take your next breath, you will have more of Him; but you will find Him in Matthew and Mark, not in television sitcoms.

2.   **Experiential sanctification:** This continues until you reach streets of gold in God's celestial city. It is the process whereby the Holy Ghost of God in you separates your mind and your body unto the Word of God; and therefore, you are submitted to the Spirit of the living God.

> **"I beseech you therefore, brethren, by the mercies of God, that ye present your bodies a living sacrifice, holy, acceptable unto God, which is your reasonable service. And be not conformed to this world: but be ye transformed by the renewing of your mind, that ye may prove what is that good, and acceptable, and perfect, will of God."**
>
> **Romans 12:1-2**

God's strength in you will do it!

But just as in salvation and positional sanctification, you must be willing to allow God to do it. Are you as willing for God to take the world out of you as you were to have Him take you out of the world?

3.   **Ultimate sanctification:** This is manifested when our bodies shall be changed – in a moment, in the twinkling of an eye. Our mortal man is going to shed its mortality and put on immortality, and this corruption is going to put on incorruptibility.

You will not reach this state until the rapture, when in an instant we are going to be changed.

> **"…it doth not yet appear what we shall be: but we know that, when he shall appear, we shall be like him; for we shall see him as he is."**
>
> 1 John 3:2

In your ultimate sanctification, you will walk up and down heavenly boulevards made out of purest gold. You will see gates made out of pearls. It will not matter if you are underneath the crusty surface of the earth in a coal mine or flying around in the space shuttle, when God gets ready to change you, to take you out of this world, you will be instantly like Him!

> **"I tell you, in that night there shall be two men in one bed; the one shall be taken, and the other shall be left. Two women shall be grinding together; the one shall be taken, and the other left. Two men shall be in the field; the one shall be taken, and the other left."**
>
> Luke 17:34-36

You will meet the Lord in the air and be with the Lord forever.

Sin Versus Sanctification

Sin – the subject we all have in common that nobody wants to talk about – stops sanctification, will drag you down in this life, and damn your eternal soul. **"For the wages of sin is death; but the gift of God is eternal life through Jesus Christ our Lord" (Romans 6:23).**

Break the chains of sin.

Get free.

The only sin God cannot forgive is unconfessed sin.

> **"If we confess our sins, he is faithful and just to forgive us our sins, and to cleanse us from all unrighteousness."**
>
> 1 John 1:9

God wants you to renounce your sins, confess them, and start the sanctification process.

> **"And the very God of peace sanctify you wholly; and I pray God your whole spirit and soul and body be preserved blameless unto the coming of our Lord Jesus Christ."**
>
> 1 Thessalonians 5:23

Maturing Through Holiness

I believe the church of Jesus Christ is growing in maturity; we are going to become young men and fathers.

> **"I write unto you, fathers, because ye have known him that is from the beginning. I write unto you, young men, because ye have overcome the wicked one. I write unto you, little children, because ye have known the Father."**
>
> 1 John 2:13

We are going to be able to say we know Him, not just that we know about Him. We are going to have a revelation of Jesus for ourselves, not just a knowledge of someone else's revelation of Him. We are going to stop trying to jump on someone else's coat tails to get our deliverance, our healing, our blessings, or our miracles.

We will talk with God in the mountain of His holiness.

> **"He that dwelleth in the secret place of the most High shall abide under the shadow of the Almighty.**

> I will say of the Lord, He is my refuge and my for-
> tress: my God; in him will I trust."
>
> **Psalm 91:1-2**

There are basic growth transitions we follow in the Word of God.

First, God calls us little children.

> **"My little children, these things write I unto you,
> that ye sin not. And if any man sin, we have an advo-
> cate with the Father, Jesus Christ the righteous."**
>
> **1 John 2:1**

> **"If we confess our sins, he is faithful and just to
> forgive us our sins, and to cleanse us from all un-
> righteousness."**
>
> **1 John 1:9**

Those promises are for little children.

After that, He said we would become young men. Young men have learned to take authority over the devil.

> **"And they overcame him by the blood of the
> Lamb, and by the word of their testimony…"**
>
> **Revelation 12:11**

Young men have been washed in the blood of Jesus and have learned to use the words of their mouths to defeat the adversary in their lives.

Beyond that, John speaks of becoming fathers.

Fathers understand who Jesus is – the Lamb slain from the foundation of the world. John said, "I call you fathers because you have known Him."

Fathers KNOW Jesus.

Even Paul prays, **"That I may know him, and the power of his resurrection…"** (Philippians 3:10).

Little children.

Young men.

Fathers!

Fruit.

Much fruit.

More fruit!

Outer court.

Inner court.

The holy of holies!

That is God's progression.

> **"Neither by the blood of goats and calves, but by his own blood he entered in once into the holy place, having obtained eternal redemption for us."**
>
> **Hebrews 9:12**

Through Jesus, we can enter the holy place, yet the church has been standing in the outer court!

Oh, a few Christians have made it into the inner court where they have washed their hands in the brass basin, and they have offered sacrifices according to Romans.

> **"I beseech you therefore, brethren, by the mercies of God, that ye present your bodies a living sacrifice, holy, acceptable unto God, which is your reasonable service. And be not conformed to this world: but be ye transformed by the renewing of your mind, that ye may prove what is that good, and acceptable, and perfect, will of God."**
>
> **Romans 12:1-2**

A few have presented their bodies a living sacrifice and have not been conformed to this world.

From the outer court and from the inner court, we have to be satisfied with sending someone else into the presence of God for us in the holy of holies. We say to our pastors, "Please, go in and talk to God for me. Pray for me. Tell God about this problem for me. And when you are finished, come back out of the holy place and tell me what God looks and sounds like.

"Tell me that His voice is as the sound of many waters; my ears ache to hear His Word. But I cannot go, for I am not sanctified. I'm unclean, and another must go for me. I have offered no sacrifice for myself, so I will try to get by on the sacrifices offered by another."

It is time we understand that God intends for each of us to experience His full anointing, His full power, and expects us to enter into the holy of holies.

> **"But ye have an unction from the Holy One, and ye know all things."**
>
> **1 John 2:20**

Do you see that?

Each of us has the spiritual inheritance to receive an anointing, an unction from the Holy Ghost! Personal sacrifices are necessary to walk in that anointing, but the unction is there for all to receive.

It is time for you to sanctify your life, free yourself from sin, and climb that spiritual mountain to receive the unction God has for you!

I submit to you that we are moving from little children to young men to full-grown fathers – from the blade to the ear to the full corn in the ear. We are growing and maturing, no longer satisfied to have a knowledge of someone else's revelation of God.

There are those who are willing to wash and cleanse themselves and offer their own sacrifices so the veil to the holiest of holies will be opened on their behalf. There are those who are hearing the wooing cry of God, "Come unto me."

God does not dwell in the outer court.

God does not dwell in the inner court.

He dwells in the holiest of holies.

We have to realize that the power of God is based upon the holiness of God. He is all powerful because He is absolutely holy. That separates Him from anything and everything else.

Look at the power Jesus walked in. Was it just because He had the Spirit without measure?

Absolutely not.

He had the Spirit without measure because He was the sanctified vessel of the Father. He went to the sacrificial altar in the holy place and washed Himself of the spirit of the world.

Jesus declared, **"...touch not the unclean thing" (2 Corinthians 6:17)**. He declared, **"...not my will, but thine, be done" (Luke 22:42)**.

The Father then pulled back the veil, and the Son walked with the Father in holiness. Though He was **"...in all points tempted like as we are, [He was] yet without sin" (Hebrews 4:15)**. He demonstrated His power over sin, releasing Himself into the very holiness of God, which became the energy behind His power.

Do you desire to have power with God?

It is not found in how high you jump in church or how loud you shout, "Amen!"

It is how you walk when your feet hit the ground. If you walk in holiness, you will have the power of God and enter the holy place.

When the priest entered into the holiest of holies, a rope was fastened around his leg. Why? Because if the proper sacrifice was not made or if any sin was still upon him, he would be slain by the purity, power, and radiance of the holiness of God!

We cry out to God, "Oh Lord, give me Your presence."

If God's presence would come upon us in the lifestyle many of us are currently living in, He would consume us.

God does not say, "Let us take the surgical scalpel and go in and find the leaven and cut it out."

God says, **"For the wages of sin is death..." (Romans 6:23)**!

The radiance of God's power annihilates sin and anything around it.

What you are reading now is true spiritual meat; it is what will challenge and mature the Body of Christ to live in holiness, releasing God's power to flood the earth like the waters cover the sea.

I pray the Holy Ghost is convicting you through this message. If you want to be filled with the Holy Ghost, if you want tongue-talking, sin-eradicating, devil-stomping power, then you are going to have to receive *all* that the Holy Ghost will do with your life.

Righteousness does not ignore sin; righteousness gives you power over all sin. Righteousness is positional; holiness is experiential. Righteousness is what God did, and holiness is what you must do. Righteousness gives you the power to be holy, to wash yourself.

The Bible says to present your bodies, renew your mind, and be transformed. He did not say He would do it for you; He said for you to do it (Romans 12:1-2).

If you do that, then you can walk into the presence of God, into the holiest of holies where God dwells. There the scales will drop from your eyes and you will see Him. There the stops will come out of your ears, and you will hear Him.

When you come out of the secret place of the holiest of holies, humanity will note, "This is a person who has been in the presence of God" (Acts 4:13).

When you come out of the holiest of holies, you will have the holy presence of God upon you.

Rather than seeking the face of God, many seek what their flesh wants. The modern Body of Christ is on a comfort quest. We seek deliverance, healings, blessings – a pampered primrose path. In seeking just for those things, we leave behind this fundamental spiritual reality: If you want to be comforted, become established, rooted and grounded in faith, growing up to **"...the measure of the stature of the fulness of Christ"** (Ephesians 4:13).

"Wherefore seeing we also are compassed about with so great a cloud of witnesses, let us lay aside every weight, and the sin which doth so easily beset

**us, and let us run with patience the race that is set
before us."**

Hebrews 12:1

It is time to leave behind the weights of sin. It is time for us to stop pursuing the kingdom of darkness and begin pursuing the kingdom of light.

We are the "John the Baptists" of our generation. John dwelt in the wilderness and ate locusts and wild honey. Let us, like John, be separate unto the Lord.

When Jesus spoke to the people concerning John, He said **"But what went ye out for to see? A man clothed in soft raiment...gorgeously appareled...**[living] **in kings' courts" (Luke 7:25).**

No!

"A friend of the world," says God, "is an enemy to the cross of Christ."

Growth Without Wires

When you set out a seedling tree, you must put a stake down around it and run a wire to it to make sure the wind does not blow it down. Then it can grow straight and strong. It needs external support until it begins to grow – then you can remove the wires.

When you pour concrete, you pour it into forms, or it will flow out of where it is supposed to be and come out something other than what it was intended to be. But when that concrete sets, you can take off the forms.

God took the forms off of the old law. He took the stakes and wires off. But some Christians were not set, and they have become something other than what their Creator intended them to be. They have used their freedom as an occasion to their flesh.

Paul essentially told the church at Thessalonica, **"I wanted to bring you a message to establish you, but I couldn't come myself. I sent Timothy to deliver it to you, so that you could become established and comforted" (1 Thessalonians 3:1-12).**

And what was that message?

"For this is the will of God, even your sanctification, that ye should abstain from fornication."

1 Thessalonians 4:3

Fornication is one of the manifestations of the lust of the flesh and will sentence man to the torment of hell. To abstain from fornication is not bondage, but freedom. To abstain from fornication means you experience FREEDOM from gonorrhea, FREEDOM from syphilis, and FREEDOM from AIDS.

You see, the holiness of God makes you free.

The Role of Grace

The grace of God, the unmerited favor of God, can free the vilest sinner. Grace can deliver the alcoholic, liberate the lesbian, free the prostitute. Grace to the believer is immeasurable, undeniable, and indestructible.

But there is something about grace you should not forget: grace cannot condemn the sinner and excuse the saint!

Before we were saved, we were told fornication was sin and that it would lead us to hell. But after we were saved, we were told fornication "is a problem," and should be treated with counseling.

Calling fornication "a problem" is not a confession of your sin; and grace cannot forgive unconfessed sin. If fornication is sin for the sinner, then it is sin for the saint!

It is time somebody told the truth.

It is time for a cleansing and a purifying of the church of Jesus Christ. It is time we become established in the holiness of God and live where the evil one cannot touch us.

I am tired of the church looking like the world, talking like the world, acting like the world, moving like the world, conducting their business like the world, and having music like the world.

By the grace of God, I pray our preachers repent on their faces before God, for they have not warned the wicked man of his wicked deeds. Humanity is dying in wickedness, and their blood is going to be required at the hands of those who did not warn them.

It is time to let the blood of Jesus Christ cleanse us from all unrighteousness.

Many Christians think no more of heading for the divorce court than they do traffic court. Some preachers openly excuse their own weakness in the flesh by telling their congregations, "It's all right to get a divorce. God just wants you to be happy." Usually, these preachers want to be divorced themselves!

As a pastor, if I tell you what you want to hear, you will like me; but if I do not tell you what God wants you to hear, God does not like it.

I would rather please God than man.

Grace cannot forgive an unrepentant heart!

Grace cannot guarantee man eternal life if he refuses to obey!

Grace cannot cancel God's law of sowing and reaping!

I have seen many ministry sermons on sowing and reaping financially, but I cannot locate one sermon on this passage of sowing and reaping:

> **"Be not deceived; God is not mocked: for whatsoever a man soweth, that shall he also reap. For he that soweth to his flesh shall of the flesh reap corruption; but he that soweth to the Spirit shall of the Spirit reap life everlasting."**
>
> **Galatians 6:7-8**

Grace cannot keep you from moral failure if you willfully choose to sin. Your sin will find you out – there is a payday someday. You may fool the preacher, and you may fool the deacon; but you cannot fool the One who sits on the throne!

Grace cannot forgive you when you do not repent.

You cannot commit fornication on Saturday night and walk into the sanctuary of God on Sunday morning and say, "Sorry, God, I failed. I'm sorry," acting like nothing much happened.

> **"...the soul that sinneth, it shall die."**
>
> **Ezekiel 18:4**

We need more preachers who will thunder out like the prophets instead of pathetic puppets.

The Body of Christ wants to be holy, to be pure, to have the power of God, to live right – but they must have a preacher.

> **"How then shall they call on him in whom they have not believed? and how shall they believe in him of whom they have not heard? and how shall they hear without a preacher?"**
>
> **Romans 10:14**

Sin Erodes

I am mad at the diabolical deception known as sin. Like a sickening cancer, it erodes the power away from the Body of Christ until the church stands on sinking sand with no solid foundation.

> **"For this cause, when I could no longer forbear, I sent to know your faith, lest by some means the tempter have tempted you, and our labour be in vain."**
>
> **1 Thessalonians 3:5**

Paul said, "I gave spiritual birth to you. You are my children; you are the apple of my eye; you are the fruit of my labor. I have heard God say, 'Bring the church warning, lest your labor be in vain and the tempter come and tempt them, and they fall away.'"

Because you are ready to go to heaven today is no guarantee you will be ready to go tomorrow. Grace is not unconditional; it is absolutely conditional.

God help us that we do not spend our lives preaching to congergations of people and call the wicked righteous. For the Bible says, **"He that saith unto the wicked, Thou art righteous; him shall the people curse" (Proverbs 24:24).**

Oh, for a people who want to hear the truth, who want to get out of the lap of sin, who want to come out from amongst the world and be separate. Oh, for a group of people who will say,

"Tell the truth. Call sin sin, call righteousness righteousness, and let us know the difference so we are not confused and deceived. Let us know the dividing line and the truth."

> **"And the very God of peace sanctify you wholly; and I pray God your whole spirit and soul and body be preserved blameless unto the coming of our Lord Jesus Christ."**
>
> 1 Thessalonians 5:23

I pray the God of peace sanctifies you.

I want you to understand that we have had so much prodding and prompting on the teaching of righteousness that we call the wicked righteous. We call sin righteous; we say immorality is acceptable. We tell our congregations to just say, "Jesus, I'm sorry."

No!

The Bible says, **"For godly sorrow worketh repentance to salvation...but the sorrow of the world worketh death"** (2 Corinthians 7:10).

Human sorrow has no convicting power, but godly sorrow makes a man or woman want to rend their clothes and sit in sackcloth and ashes, crying with tears of repentance, "My God, forgive me! I am unworthy, for I have sinned."

Calls – or Conviction?

I get worried about the condition of the church when altar calls are given so flippantly that people react as though they were joining the local country club. "Just come on down and shake my hand," they are told. "That's a beautiful smile you have. Yes, we're so glad to have you today. Yes, we're so glad that you have accepted Jesus now. Amen."

Next, the "convert" is told to sign a roll book, so they sign their name. Then, they go home and sip their wine, watch their pornography, tell dirty jokes, cheat on their taxes, and lie to their wives. They have every immoral thought imaginable running across the tapestry of their mental reasoning. They are full of envy, strife, emulation, heresy, sedition, and ungodly ambition.

Yet, we tell them they are saved!

God help your sin-sick soul, preacher; you need salvation yourself. You need to find a place in God and say, "I have sought to please the people and not to please God. From this moment forward, I'm going to be a preacher of righteousness, and I'm going to tell the truth."

Do you want the presence of God in your life?

Do you want to dwell in the secret place of the Most High?

Do you want the glory of God on your life?

Do you want to be in a position with God that when cancer attacks, you can say, "No you don't, Devil! Get your hands off the property of God," and it goes?

The way to these things is to enter into the holy presence of God, to live holy, and to be established in the things of God – sanctified wholly, set apart, completely consecrated and dedicated unto God.

When God first started birthing this revelation in my heart, I asked Him, "Lord, help me to write this. God, I don't want to write about fornication, adultery, uncleanness, and lasciviousness. I don't want to talk about emulation, strife, heresy, sedition, murder, and reveling. I don't want to write about that denomination spirit and that clique spirit."

Even in the time of Paul, Christians were saying, "I am of Paul; I am of Cephas; I am of Christ" (1 Corinthians 1:12).

Paul challenged them, **"Is Christ divided? was Paul crucified for you? or were ye baptized in the name of Paul?" (v. 13).**

The denominational spirit that says, "We're the only ones making it. We're the only holy ones. We're the only ones who have the truth" is of the devil.

We are all in the Body of Christ together – those who have been blood-bought, blood-washed, and God-forgiven.

"This poor man cried, and the Lord heard him,
and saved him out of all his troubles."

Psalm 34:6

Endnote

[1] Adapted from Walter B. Knight, *Knight's Master Book of New Illustrations* (Grand Rapids: Eerdman's Printing Company, 1986), p. 624.

Your Holiness Tool Kit

Here Are the Tools, the Spiritual Hammer and Nails, You Need to Biblically Repair and Restore the Holiness Plank in Your Life.

I. Sin Before the Age of Accountability

Matthew 18:1 At the same time came the disciples unto Jesus, saying, Who is the greatest in the kingdom of heaven?

v. 2 And Jesus called a little child unto him, and set him in the midst of them,

v. 3 And said, Verily I say unto you, Except ye be converted, and become as little children, ye shall not enter into the kingdom of heaven.

v. 4 Whosoever therefore shall humble himself as this little child, the same is greatest in the kingdom of heaven.

v. 5 And whoso shall receive one such little child in my name receiveth me.

v. 6 But whoso shall offend one of these little ones which believe in me, it were better for him that a millstone were hanged about his neck, and that he were drowned in the depth of the sea.

Matthew 19:13 Then were there brought unto him little children, that he should put his hands on them, and pray: and the disciples rebuked them.

v. 14 But Jesus said, Suffer little children, and forbid them not, to come unto me: for of such is the kingdom of heaven.

v. 15 And he laid his hands on them, and departed thence.

Luke 18:15 And they brought unto him also infants, that he would touch them: but when his disciples saw it, they rebuked them.

v. 16 But Jesus called them unto him, and said, Suffer little children to come unto me, and forbid them not: for of such is the kingdom of God.

v. 17 Verily I say unto you, Whosoever shall not receive the kingdom of God as a little child shall in no wise enter therein.

Mark 10:13 And they brought young children to him, that he should touch them: and his disciples rebuked those that brought them.

v. 14 But when Jesus saw it, he was much displeased, and said unto them, Suffer the little children to come unto me, and forbid them not: for of such is the kingdom of God.

v. 15 Verily I say unto you, Whosoever shall not receive the kingdom of God as a little child, he shall not enter therein.

v. 16 And he took them up in his arms, put his hands upon them, and blessed them.

II.   Sin, the Universal Horror

Genesis 6:5 And God saw that the wickedness of man was great in the earth, and that every imagination of the thoughts of his heart was only evil continually.

Genesis 6:11 The earth also was corrupt before God, and the earth was filled with violence.

v. 12 And God looked upon the earth, and, behold, it was corrupt; for all flesh had corrupted his way upon the earth.

Genesis 13:13 But the men of Sodom were wicked and sinners before the Lord exceedingly.

Deuteronomy 32:5 They have corrupted themselves, their spot is not the spot of his children: they are a perverse and crooked generation.

Psalm 14:1 The fool hath said in his heart, There is no God. They are corrupt, they have done abominable works, there is none that doeth good.

v. 2 The Lord looked down from heaven upon the children of men, to see if there were any that did understand, and seek God.

v. 3 They are all gone aside, they are all together become filthy: there is none that doeth good, no, not one.

Psalm 53:1 The fool hath said in his heart, There is no God. Corrupt are they, and have done abominable iniquity: there is none that doeth good.

v. 2 God looked down from heaven upon the children of men, to see if there were any that did understand, that did seek God.

v. 3 Every one of them is gone back: they are altogether become filthy; there is none that doeth good, no, not one.

Ecclesiastes 7:27 Behold, this have I found, saith the preacher, counting one by one, to find out the account:

v. 28 Which yet my soul seeketh, but I find not: one man among a thousand have I found; but a woman among all those have I not found.

v. 29 Lo, this only have I found, that God hath made man upright; but they have sought out many inventions.

Ecclesiastes 8:11 Because sentence against an evil work is not executed speedily, therefore the heart of the sons of men is fully set in them to do evil.

Jeremiah 2:29 Wherefore will ye plead with me? ye all have transgressed against me, saith the Lord.

Jeremiah 2:35 Yet thou sayest, Because I am innocent, surely his anger shall turn from me. Behold, I will plead with thee, because thou sayest, I have not sinned.

Mark 7:20 And he said, That which cometh out of the man, that defileth the man.

v 21 For from within, out of the heart of men, proceed evil thoughts, adulteries, fornications, murders,

v 22 Thefts, covetousness, wickedness, deceit, lasciviousness, an evil eye, blasphemy, pride, foolishness:

v 23 All these evil things come from within, and defile the man.

John 5:45 Do not think that I will accuse you to the Father: there is one that accuseth you, even Moses, in whom ye trust.

Romans 3:9 What then? are we better than they? No, in no wise: for we have before proved both Jews and Gentiles, that they are all under sin;

v. 10 As it is written, There is none righteous, no, not one:

v. 11 There is none that understandeth, there is none that seeketh after God.

v. 12 They are all gone out of the way, they are together become unprofitable; there is none that doeth good, no, not one.

1 John 5:19 And we know that we are of God, and the whole world lieth in wickedness.

III.   Sin, Guilt Universal

Isaiah 64:6 But we are all as an unclean thing, and all our righteousnesses are as filthy rags; and we all do fade as a leaf; and our iniquities, like the wind, have taken us away.

Romans 3:19 Now we know that what things soever the law saith, it saith to them who are under the law: that every mouth may be stopped, and all the world may become guilty before God.

Romans 3:23 For all have sinned, and come short of the glory of God;

Romans 5:12 Wherefore, as by one man sin entered into the world, and death by sin; and so death passed upon all men, for that all have sinned:

Romans 5:14 Nevertheless death reigned from Adam to Moses, even over them that had not sinned after the similitude of Adam's transgression, who is the figure of him that was to come.

Galatians 3:29 And if ye be Christ's, then are ye Abraham's seed, and heirs according to the promise.

IV.   Sin of the Flesh

Isaiah 59:3 For your hands are defiled with blood, and your fingers with iniquity; your lips have spoken lies, your tongue hath muttered perverseness.

v. 4 None calleth for justice, nor any pleadeth for truth: they trust in vanity, and speak lies; they conceive mischief, and bring forth iniquity.

v. 5 They hatch cockatrice' eggs, and weave the spider's web: he that eateth of their eggs dieth, and that which is crushed breaketh out into a viper.

v. 6 Their webs shall not become garments, neither shall they cover themselves with their works: their works are works of iniquity, and the act of violence is in their hands.

v. 7 Their feet run to evil, and they make haste to shed innocent blood: their thoughts are thoughts of iniquity; wasting and destruction are in their paths.

v. 8 The way of peace they know not; and there is no judgment in their goings: they have made them crooked paths: whosoever goeth therein shall not know peace.

v. 9 Therefore is judgment far from us, neither doth justice overtake us: we wait for light, but behold obscurity; for brightness, but we walk in darkness.

v. 10 We grope for the wall like the blind, and we grope as if we had no eyes: we stumble at noon day as in the night; we are in desolate places as dead men.

v. 11 We roar all like bears, and mourn sore like doves: we look for judgment, but there is none; for salvation, but it is far off from us.

v. 12 For our transgressions are multiplied before thee, and our sins testify against us: for our transgressions are with us; and as for our iniquities, we know them;

v. 13 In transgressing and lying against the Lord, and departing away from our God, speaking oppression and revolt, conceiving and uttering from the heart words of falsehood.

v. 14 And judgment is turned away backward, and justice standeth afar off: for truth is fallen in the street, and equity cannot enter.

Proverbs 6:16 These six things doth the Lord hate: yea, seven are an abomination unto him:

v. 17 A proud look, a lying tongue, and hands that shed innocent blood,

v. 18 An heart that deviseth wicked imaginations, feet that be swift in running to mischief.

John 8:41 Ye do the deeds of your father. Then said they to him, We be not born of fornication; we have one Father, even God.

Romans 1:29 Being filled with all unrighteousness, fornication, wickedness, covetousness, maliciousness; full of envy, murder, debate, deceit, malignity; whisperers,

v. 30 Backbiters, haters of God, despiteful, proud, boasters, inventors of evil things, disobedient to parents,

v. 31 Without understanding, covenantbreakers, without natural affection, implacable, unmerciful:

v. 32 Who knowing the judgment of God, that they which commit such things are worthy of death, not only do the same, but have pleasure in them that do them.

Romans 3:13 Their throat is an open sepulchre; with their tongues they have used deceit; the poison of asps is under their lips:

v. 14 Whose mouth is full of cursing and bitterness:

v. 15 Their feet are swift to shed blood.

V.   Jesus Deals with Sin

John 4:16 Jesus saith unto her, Go, call thy husband, and come hither.

v. 17 The woman answered and said, I have no husband. Jesus said unto her, Thou hast well said, I have no husband:

v. 18 For thou hast had five husbands; and he whom thou now hast is not thy husband: in that saidst thou truly.

John 8:3 And the scribes and Pharisees brought unto him a woman taken in adultery; and when they had set her in the midst,

v. 4 They say unto him, Master, this woman was taken in adultery, in the very act.

v. 5   Now Moses in the law commanded us, that such should be stoned: but what sayest thou?

v. 6 This they said, tempting him, that they might have to accuse him. But Jesus stooped down, and with his finger wrote on the ground, as though he heard them not.

v. 7 So when they continued asking him, he lifted up himself, and said unto them, He that is without sin among you, let him first cast a stone at her.

v. 8   And again he stooped down, and wrote on the ground.

v. 9   And they which heard it, being convicted by their own conscience, went out one by one, beginning at the eldest, even unto the last: and Jesus was left alone, and the woman standing in the midst.

v. 10 When Jesus had lifted up himself, and saw none but the woman, he said unto her, Woman, where are those thine accusers? hath no man condemned thee?

v. 11 She said, No man, Lord. And Jesus said unto her, Neither do I condemn thee: go, and sin no more.

Mark 2:3 And they come unto him, bringing one sick of the palsy, which was borne of four.

v. 4   And when they could not come nigh unto him for the press, they uncovered the roof where he was: and when they had broken it up, they let down the bed wherein the sick of the palsy lay.

v. 5   When Jesus saw their faith, he said unto the sick of the palsy, Son, thy sins be forgiven thee.

v. 6   But there were certain of the scribes sitting there, and reasoning in their hearts,

v. 7   Why doth this man thus speak blasphemies? who can forgive sins but God only?

v. 8   And immediately when Jesus perceived in his spirit that they so reasoned within themselves, he said unto them, Why reason ye these things in your hearts?

v. 9 Whether is it easier to say to the sick of the palsy, Thy sins be forgiven thee; or to say, Arise, and take up thy bed, and walk?

v. 10 But that ye may know that the Son of man hath power on earth to forgive sins, (he saith to the sick of the palsy,)

v. 11. I say unto thee, Arise, and take up thy bed, and go thy way into thine house.

Matthew 18:21 Then came Peter to him, and said, Lord, how oft shall my brother sin against me, and I forgive him? till seven times?

v. 22 Jesus saith unto him, I say not unto thee, Until seven times: but, Until seventy times seven.

VI.   Sin of the Spirit

James 1:8 A double minded man is unstable in all his ways.

James 4:8 Draw nigh to God, and he will draw nigh to you. Cleanse your hands, ye sinners; and purify your hearts, ye double minded.

Matthew 13:13 Therefore speak I to them in parables: because they seeing see not; and hearing they hear not, neither do they understand.

v. 14 And in them is fulfilled the prophecy of Esaias, which saith, By hearing ye shall hear, and shall not understand; and seeing ye shall see, and shall not perceive:

v. 15 For this people's heart is waxed gross, and their ears are dull of hearing, and their eyes they have closed; lest at any time they should see with their eyes, and hear with their ears, and should understand with their heart, and should be converted, and I should heal them.

1 Corinthians 15:34 Awake to righteousness, and sin not; for some have not the knowledge of God: I speak this to your shame.

2 Peter 2:12 But these, as natural brute beasts, made to be taken and destroyed, speak evil of the things that they understand not; and shall utterly perish in their own corruption.

Jude 10 But these speak evil of those things which they know not: but what they know naturally, as brute beasts, in those things they corrupt themselves.

VII.   Sin's Punishment

Exodus 32:9 And the Lord said unto Moses, I have seen this people, and, behold, it is a stiffnecked people:

v. 10 Now therefore let me alone, that my wrath may wax hot against them, and that I may consume them: and I will make of thee a great nation.

Deuteronomy 9:8 Also in Horeb ye provoked the Lord to wrath, so that the Lord was angry with you to have destroyed you.

Deuteronomy 9:22 And at Taberah, and at Massah, and at Kibroth-hatta'avah, ye provoked the Lord to wrath.

Romans 1:8 First, I thank my God through Jesus Christ for you all, that your faith is spoken of throughout the whole world.

James 4:4 Ye adulterers and adulteresses, know ye not that the friendship of the world is enmity with God? whosoever therefore will be a friend of the world is the enemy of God.

Jeremiah 8:20 The harvest is past, the summer is ended, and we are not saved.

Matthew 7:23 And then will I profess unto them, I never knew you: depart from me, ye that work iniquity.

Matthew 11:23 And thou, Capernaum, which art exalted unto heaven, shalt be brought down to hell: for if the mighty works, which have been done in thee, had been done in Sodom, it would have remained until this day.

v. 24 But I say unto you, That it shall be more tolerable for the land of Sodom in the day of judgment, than for thee.

VIII.   Salvation, the Answer to Sin

Romans 5:15 But not as the offence, so also is the free gift. For if through the offence of one many be dead, much more the grace of God, and the gift by grace, which is by one man, Jesus Christ, hath abounded unto many.

v. 16 And not as it was by one that sinned, so is the gift: for the judgment was by one to condemnation, but the free gift is of many offences unto justification.

v. 17 For if by one man's offence death reigned by one; much more they which receive abundance of grace and of the gift of righteousness shall reign in life by one, Jesus Christ.)

v. 18 Therefore as by the offence of one judgment came upon all men to condemnation; even so by the righteousness of one the free gift came upon all men unto justification of life.

v. 19 For as by one man's disobedience many were made sinners, so by the obedience of one shall many be made righteous.

v. 20 Moreover the law entered, that the offence might abound. But where sin abounded, grace did much more abound:

v. 21 That as sin hath reigned unto death, even so might grace reign through righteousness unto eternal life by Jesus Christ our Lord.

2 Corinthians 5:14 For the love of Christ constraineth us; because we thus judge, that if one died for all, then were all dead.

PLANK TWO

**Restoring True Repentance
to the Body of Christ**

PLANK TWO

Restoring True Repentance to the Body of Christ

Why are Men Lost?

A fellow said to me on the train one day, "Oh, you preachers make me sick."

"I am not a preacher," I replied. "I wish I were. I don't know enough."

He said, I don't care what you are. You Christians are always talking about a man going to hell because Adam sinned."

"No," I said, "you will never go to hell because Adam sinned. You will go to hell because you refuse the remedy provided for Adam's sin. Don't you go crying about something that has absolutely been taken care of. If you go to hell you will go over the broken Body of Jesus Christ who died to keep you out."

> – From The Double Cure
> By Melvin E. Trotter[1]

Last Chance

Quite some years ago, Bishop Phillips Brooks became quite ill and would see no visitors. When Robert Ingersoll, the agnostic, heard his friend was sick, he called at his home to see him and was admitted at once.

"I appreciate this very much," said Mr. Ingersoll, "but why do you see me when you deny yourself to all your friends?"

"It's this way," answered the bishop. "I feel confident of seeing my other friends in the next world, but this may be my last chance to see you."

> – Emory G. Young
> in Coronet[2]

New Life After Newgate

One day, Charles Hadden Spurgeon, a great Baptist preacher of the nineteenth century, was walking past Newgate prison in London.

In the nineteenth century, children were frequently sent to prison for failure to pay a debt or for stealing food.

As Dr. Spurgeon was walking, a young lad doing cartwheels crashed into him. Picking himself up and dusting off his clothes, Dr. Spurgeon indignantly chastised the boy.

The young man, at the point of tears, said to Dr. Spurgeon, "If you had just been released from prison, you would be happy, too."

– Source Unknown

The Gateway to Hell Is Open Wide

In America, there are millions of sinners who are cutting their grass today with no consciousness of God. They are jogging around the park with no consciousness of eternity. They are going to the latest movie with no consciousness of heaven. They are skiing on the nearest lake with no consciousness of hell.

You personally know several families that are only one heartbeat away from hell!

You know neighbors who are going to hell.

You know relatives who are going to hell.

Billions of people are destined for hell unless someone tells them about the need for repentance and the acceptance of Jesus Christ as their Savior!

Satan has stolen true repentance from the gospel bridge!

The devil has convinced this generation of Christians that it is far more important to go to another Bible study, to attend another Saturday seminar, to continue to be blessed, blessed, blessed – than to share the gospel of Jesus Christ with the lost souls living right next door to them!

I honestly believe there are only two reasons people are not repenting and being saved in our churches today.

Number One: We Do Not Bring Them

It seems we feel that God certainly understands we have no time to think of our neighbors and family who are one heartbeat from hell. We are too busy with other more important matters of the modern church, such as our theological self-help programs of spiritual humanism and our bank checks with little doves on them.

We are too busy being "bumper-sticker Christians," void of any significant power or anointing that might reach this suffering planet. It is a sorry spectacle!

We keep running to the house of God to find out what else He has for us. We are concerned only about ourselves, blinded by our own fleshly desires to the needs of a suffering humanity held captive by Satan.

I declare to you, we have about all we are going to get until we let go of what we have. The process of life is the process of exchange.

God cannot pour more into us until we let some out.

We must take back what the devil has stolen – an immediate URGENCY to win lost souls to the kingdom of God!

Number Two: We Need More Salvation Preaching

It takes preaching to get people saved.

We cannot bring people into church and teach them a little Bible lesson or a little triviality of gospel truth and expect them to flood to the altar. Someone must tell them that hell and heaven are still realities! They are not just places in a writer's song or a poet's poem.

Someone is going to have to preach the gospel of Jesus Christ in power!

> **"And my speech and my preaching was not with enticing words of man's wisdom, but in demonstration of the Spirit and of power."**
> **1 Corinthians 2:4**

> **"For after that in the wisdom of God the world by wisdom knew not God, it pleased God by the foolishness of preaching to save them that believe."**
> **1 Corinthians 1:21**

The time has come for our preachers to share the entire gospel, never being ashamed to preach the realities of heaven and hell, or of sin and its devastation.

God's Guarantee

"For God so loved the world, that he gave his only begotten Son, that whosoever believeth in him should not perish, but have everlasting life."

John 3:16

I have God's Word on my salvation. I will not allow Satan to soil or adulterate that Word. There are signs posted in my spirit that say, "No Trespassing." The angels of God garrison this stronghold.

I will keep this Word, for it is my life.

In Exodus 25:17-20, God commanded Moses to make two golden cherubims to overshadow the mercy seat which would go above the ark. They would protect and keep it.

In Genesis 3:24, God placed cherubims and a flaming sword to keep the way to the tree of life. The Hebrew word for "keep" is almost identical to the Greek word. As a matter of fact, the Greek Septuagint (the Greek translation of the Old Testament) uses the same word for "keep" as in John 8:51:

"Verily, verily, I say unto you, If a man keep my saying, he shall never see death."

Jewish history and tradition teach us that when Adam and Eve sinned in the Garden, God made an altar at the gate to Eden and there sacrificed the animals He killed to clothe Adam and Eve. The cherubims were placed at this gate above the altar to protect and keep the only access sinful man had to enter God's presence.

Remember, God defines death as separation from Him; hence, life was meant to be in His presence.

Salvation Is by the Blood

A young preacher decided to start a church in a small town. In this particular town there was an agnostic who ardently believed, "If there is a God, He certainly does not care anything about the affairs of men. He is so far removed you cannot get in touch with Him, and He obviously does not want to get in touch with me."

Every time a new church where the power of God was displayed would start up in this town, that agnostic would show up at the church, spew his particular beliefs, and usually cause such a negative reaction that the church would ultimately shut down and die.

Well, even though the young pastor had heard about this agnostic, he selected this particular town anyway and immediately started preaching a gospel of thunder, the gospel of Jesus Christ, telling people that Jesus died so men could be free.

One day, right in the middle of this young man's message, the town agnostic came running down the center aisle of the church. He leaped right up on the platform, pointed his finger at the young preacher, and declared, "What this man teaches is all a lie. Sir, you are nothing more than a heretic and a fake."

When the agnostic started talking, the young preacher calmly reached into his pulpit and took out a plump orange. He handed the orange to that agnostic and said, "Sir, peel this orange."

The agnostic grew angry and replied in rage, "I'm not going to peel that orange."

The congregation shouted, "Peel it!" So, he started peeling the orange, growing angrier with every strip he peeled.

Finally, the orange was stripped.

"Now, separate the orange into sections," the preacher calmly continued.

Well, by now the agnostic was just fuming. "I'm not going to do it," he declared.

Once again, the congregation yelled. "Separate it!" they commanded.

The agnostic once again complied and separated the orange, section by section, and then set it on the pulpit. The preacher picked up the first slice of that orange and began to eat it. He let a little bit of the juice run down the side of his face; he savored every bite of that orange.

He then picked up the next section of the orange and repeated the process until the orange was totally gone.

The young preacher then took out his handkerchief, wiped off his mouth, and said to the agnostic, "Now, was that a good orange or not?"

By this time, the agnostic was so angry it seemed as though flames were shooting our from his eyes.

"How would I know," he screamed. I never tasted the stupid orange."

"Well, how would you know how good my God is?" the preacher retorted. "After all, you have never tasted Him, either!"

That was the end of that agnostic's influence in that little town.

Shout Salvation From the Housetops!

If you have ever tasted of the Lord and known His goodness, then shout the news! If you do not like exciting worship, avoid heaven – believe me, there will be a lot of shouting in heaven.

We will shout that we have laid our burdens down.

We will shout that we made it all the way.

We will shout that we are free forever.

> **"Cry aloud, spare not, lift up thy voice like a trumpet, and shew my people their transgression, and the house of Jacob their sins."**
>
> **Isaiah 58:1**

John the Baptist lifted his voice "like a trumpet." On the face of the earth today, there is a group of people who will herald in the second advent of the Son of God, just as John heralded in the first.

The world has declared that the church is dead.

There has been a seeming silence of the prophetic voice of God. We have been lulled to sleep by the cadencing creeds of creation. We have listened to the doctrines of men. We have listened to "pulpit puppeteers" who have a form of godliness but deny the power thereof (2 Timothy 3:5), spewing out their doctrines of philosophic religiosity and secular humanism on the church of Jesus Christ.

They have said there is nothing to the blood.

They have declared there is nothing to the Bible. Some even announce that the Bible has lost all hold on the leaders of thought and is destined to become one of the great curiosities of the past.

New modern thinkers claim that "Thus saith the Lord" is an outworn and irrelevant phrase that means nothing in today's society, that it is as outdated as the ancient medicine man with his painted face and exotic incantations.

I beg to differ with these new thinkers. My life is based on the infallible, inerrant, ever-living, undying, unchanging reality of the Word of God.

They say there is nothing to the blood.

But the Bible says it is only the blood that can reach out from glory and into the gutter and save the alcoholic from his despair!

If I could line up those who have been rescued by the blood spilled on that lonely hill called Golgotha, the line would stretch from the earth to the moon – and back! With the splashing of every drop of that blood, the cry rises up towards heaven, declaring, "We are free, we are free, we are free at last!"

I could line up prostitutes rescued by the blood, fevered brows that it has cooled. I could line up those once bound by cancer. I could circumnavigate the globe and find millions of Christians who once had no hope until the blood broke through the chains of their darkness with the dawning of a new day.

There is only one hope for humanity, and it is the blood of Jesus Christ.

When Christ suffered the penalty of your sin, when the weight of your sin was laid upon Him on Calvary's mountain, when His flesh hung from that cross, when God allowed Him to be slain for your sins and mine, God made reconciliation possible – once and for all.

There is no salvation in a Shinto shrine, a Hindu cow, or a Buddhist temple. There is no salvation in a New Age guru licking a crystal. You can lick it until your tongue falls out, but that crystal will never save your soul! When the unlocked wheels of time carry you into the presence of a holy God, He will ask you one question: "What did you do with My Son, Jesus?"

This is God talking, the Master of the universe, the holy God that sits on the circumstances of the earth and stretches out the heavens like a canvas tent under which to dwell.

This is God asking, "Whom shall you compare Me to? There is none like Me. For where were you when I framed the worlds, and with whom did I take counsel? Who instructed Me in righteousness, for I am the Holy One of Israel?"

Where were you when He spread out the earth and set the world spinning on its axis?

It is this God, this one God, who declared there is salvation in no other name under heaven than the name of Jesus. He did not say there was salvation only through the name of the Baptists, or in the name of the Methodists, or the Presbyterians, or the Church of God, or in the name of the Assembly of God.

He said there is salvation in no other name than the name of Jesus. **"…there is none other name under heaven given among men, whereby we must be saved** [except the name of Jesus Christ of Nazareth]" **(Acts 4:12).**

I am tired of religion. I am overwhelmingly, indescribably tired of people filing into churches day after day, week after week, going through the rudiments of religion, as sure for hell as if they were already there, with no one to stand up and tell them the truth.

The skeptic says, "There's nothing to the blood." He says, "There's nothing to the atonement of Jesus Christ."

But the writer of Hebrews declares that there is no remission of sins without the shedding of blood (Hebrews 9:22). There is only one way to receive salvation, and that is to recognize you are a sinner in need of the blood of a Savior.

It Is Time for a Dying Race to Look to a Resurrected Savior!

It does not matter if you come to church wearing a new silk necktie and the finest suit you can buy. It does not matter if you give $10,000 a week to your favorite local charity or church. You can drive the finest and fastest car on the planet, have diamond rings on your fingers and gold on your toes. You can climb the largest corporate ladder of success, and have everyone know your name (even have the entire office staff go silent when you walk through the door) – and it will not make one bit of difference to God.

God does not care if you have servants when you come in and servants when you go out, if you have someone to mix your coffee and stir your tea. God does not care about your bulging bank balance or the size of your biceps.

To God, you can be the lowest person living on the streets, without a dollar for food or a place to put your head, and He will love you just as much as if you were an international celebrity of worldwide acclaim!

God sent His Son to save from the uppermost to the guttermost.

Every sinner who cries out, "Lord God, I am a sinner in need of a Savior" can find the redeeming, life-changing, eternity-changing power of Jesus Christ.

We must restore this salvation message to the Body of Christ. This plank must be put back in the bridge. Satan has tried to steal it, but we are putting it back.

I am talking about the Bible, not a religious, humanistic perspective. God has some men coming out of the wilderness; the world thought they were lost. We have been lulled to sleep by the "pulpit jockeys" with their oratory and philosophy. We have been lulled to sleep by the eloquence of the doctrines of men. They have told us we are all right, when inside we are full of dead men's bones. They have said, "Just dress up and try to be nice." They have said, "Just come to my church and give a little money every now and then, and you will surely make it." They have said, "It's all right, just go to church on Easter and Christmas." They have said, "All truth is relative."

The only truth that counts in this world is this: Jesus Christ of Nazareth is the only begotten Son of God – He came from heaven to this earth – lived a godly life – shed His sinless blood on an old rugged cross to free humanity from their sin – was buried and on the third day rose again from the dead, victorious over death and hell.

And because He lives, you can live also!

We have some modern day John the Baptists coming out of the wilderness; they have been eating locusts and wild honey.

Do you know what that means?

It means they are not bought by anything but the blood; no one owns their soul; they are not waiting on orders from their denominational headquarters to tell them what they should preach and how they should act.

They are men who have been to the mountain of God.

They are not merely reciting some religious rhetoric or ear-tickling, people-pleasing, conscience-soothing gospel. They have climbed the alpine summit of the glory of God and sat and communed with the Most High at a table spread with heavenly fare.

They have heard the voice of God.

They have been to the mountain and watched the lightning flash out of dark-throated storm clouds; they have heard and felt the thunderous quaking of God.

They are coming out of the wilderness all over America and all over the world; and the scheming hordes of hell are being silenced as these spiritual giants come out of the wilderness crying, "Repent, for the kingdom of God is at hand."

Will you join their royal ranks?

I am tired of people attempting to manipulate your mind with the lies of religion. I am tired of the dead ends of denominational disasters. Jesus said, **"Making the word of God of none effect through your tradition…" (Mark 7:13).**

Neckties, pretty dresses, and sanctuaries will not save you.

> **"John did baptize in the wilderness, and preach the baptism of repentance for the remission of sins."**
> **Mark 1:4**

John baptized with water unto repentance.

Many are duped to think they have repented, when all they have really done is apologize. They have yet to repent; repentance is turning around. When there is true repentance, God sends a time of refreshing; and there is joy unspeakable and full of glory. If each day you are fighting sin, trying to be good and failing, and apologizing – then you need repentance.

If you will repent and die to your sin, you will get victory over it.

The prophet Isaiah declared that, **"…thou shalt call thy walls Salvation, and thy gates Praise" (Isaiah 60:18).** After peering at earth from the far reaches of outer space, one of our astronauts said, "The only man-made object we could see was the Great Wall of China." The Great Wall of China was and is a monument to the wars and violence that have been a part of the human experience since Adam's sin in the Garden of Eden.

God is calling us to build something more enduring than the Great Wall of China. By impacting lives for Jesus, we are being called upon to build a monument that will forever be seen from timeless reaches of eternity. We are called to build walls of salvation. God is calling us to restore the reality of salvation through the blood of Jesus to the Body of Christ.

Guilty but Blameless

One of the hardest things in the world is to be convinced of a lie – because it goes against the grain of reality.

Some people think it is hard to believe God; but God does not lie, so it is easy to believe Him. It is easy to be convinced of the truth, and when you **"...know the truth...the truth shall make you free"** (John 8:32).

God is a liberator, not a liar. He will set you free to live right.

> **"I have not written unto you because ye know not the truth, but because ye know it, and that no lie is of the truth."**
>
> **1 John 2:21**

It is hard to be convinced of a lie. That is the reason alcoholics keep going back to the bottle. The bottle tells them, "I will satisfy your thirst," but it never does. Adulterers repeat the sin over and over because they are searching for the lie it promises: "Have sex with this particular person, and you will be happy." Since the lie's promise was not delivered the first time, adulterers keep trying, hoping eventually the lie will be fulfilled.

It is hard to be convinced of a lie.

Abraham, on the other hand, said, "I am fully persuaded that what God has promised, God is able to perform."

Now, that is truth; that is reality.

Jesus said, "Woman, you offer Me a drink; let Me give you a drink. And when I give you a drink, you'll never thirst again."

> **"But whosoever drinketh of the water that I shall give him shall never thirst; but the water that I shall give him shall be in him a well of water springing up into everlasting life."**
>
> **John 4:14**

The truth will convince you; it will persuade you; and the Word is truth.

You can only be fully persuaded of the truth. You cannot be fully persuaded of a lie unless God turns you over to a reprobate mind. As long as you still want what is right, you do not have a reprobate mind. You only have a reprobate mind when white looks black and black looks white, right looks wrong and wrong looks right. A reprobate is a person on whom the truth has no effect, because they have believed a lie.

> **"Now as Jannes and Jambres withstood Moses, so do these also resist the truth: men of corrupt minds, reprobate concerning the faith."**
>
> **2 Timothy 3:8**

Most of us are not as full of doubt as we think we are. In fact, we are full of faith!

The Bible says, **"...God hath dealt to every man the measure of faith" (Romans 12:3).** You have been sold a lie, conned into believing you do not have any faith. Romans 12:3 guarantees that faith has been imparted to you and righteousness has been imparted to you. It is hard for you to be unholy; you can do it, but it is difficult – **"...the way of transgressors is hard" (Proverbs 13:15).**

We think we have to fight to be holy. God's Word, however, says, **"And the very God of peace sanctify you wholly; and I pray God your whole spirit and soul and body be preserved blameless unto the coming of our Lord Jesus Christ" (1 Thessalonians 5:23).**

He did not say "guiltless;" He said "blameless."

You cannot be held blameless unless you have first been found guilty.

"Blameless" is a word that is rarely used in our court systems anymore. The jury finds a man "guilty," but the judge can declare him "blameless." That means he committed the crime, but we are not going to sentence him for it.

As a sinner, you are guilty; but God looks at the blood of Jesus Christ and holds you blameless. By the blood of Christ and your faith in the finished work of Calvary, you are held blameless. You are just as guilty as a fox in a chicken coop, and you know it. You have feathers stuck to your jowls and blood on your chin.

You are guilty.

Paul prayed that your whole spirit and soul and body be preserved blameless. That is how we receive conviction, not condemnation. Conviction drives us to the mercy seat where we say, "God, I'm guilty." But the Son, seated at the right hand of the Father, points to the blood on the mercy seat. By the blood, God, the eternal Judge, declares, "Yes, you are guilty; but I hold you blameless. I'm not going to hold your sin to your charge."

Abraham believed God for his son; and it was imputed unto him for righteousness, because he believed the truth. God gave Abraham this promise:

> **"...Sarah thy wife shall bear thee a son indeed; and thou shalt call his name Isaac: and I will establish my covenant with him for an everlasting covenant, and with his seed after him."**
>
> **Genesis 17:19**

God gave this promise to Abraham when he was a hundred years old and his wife was ninety!

In the natural, this was a promise that made no sense. Abraham could not logically see it happening, could not see, feel, touch, taste, or smell any tangible evidence to prove the promise.

Yet, he believed the truth of the Word. He was not going to believe a lie. He did not consider his own body now sexually dead, nor did he fret about the deadness of Sarah's womb (Genesis 18:11).

God said, "You're going to have a baby. And by his seed all nations of the earth shall be blessed."

Sarah laughed, but Abraham believed God. Abraham had faith in God's Word.

> **"Is any thing too hard for the Lord? At the time appointed I will return unto thee, according to the time of life, and Sarah shall have a son."**
>
> **Genesis 18:14**

Abraham hoped against hope. He knew that when things seem hopeless, that is when you are ready to hope. Hope says, "Here's something to believe in." Hope is the beginning of faith, and faith **"…calleth those things which be not as though they were" (Romans 4:17).**

Faith sees what cannot be seen, hears what cannot be heard. Faith changes you into a human being who can believe what cannot be believed, who can see what cannot be seen, and who can hear what cannot be heard.

Faith is on the inside of you right now.

Faith for what?

To believe.

To believe what?

The truth of God's Word.

Abraham said, "My body says it can't happen, but God said it is going to be so."

> **"And the scripture was fulfilled which saith, Abraham believed God, and it was imputed unto him for righteousness: and he was called the Friend of God."**
>
> **James 2:23**

The Truth of Sanctification

When you are born again, you are positionally sanctified. You were once in the kingdom of darkness, now you are in the kingdom of light.

Let me ask you a question. If you are born again, can you become MORE born again?

Of course not. You did not do anything to earn the experience, so how could you possibly earn MORE?

"For by grace are ye saved through faith; and that not of yourselves: it is the gift of God: Not of works, lest any man should boast."

Ephesians 2:8-9

You cried out, "God, I'm a sinner."

God replied, "That's all right; I'm a Savior."

You cried out, "God, I'm weak."

He lovingly answered, "That's all right; I'm strong."

You tearfully told Him, "God, You don't understand. I'm so unworthy."

"That's all right; I'm worthy," He reassured you.

"But God, You don't want me; I'm unholy and sick," you continued.

"I'm holy," He said, "And I'm a God that heals your infirmities."

"But God, I'm broke," you told Him.

"That's okay," He replied, "I'm rich. I own the cattle on a thousand hills. You just give Me what you have, and I'll give you what I have. We'll come into a blood covenant relationship. What I have will be yours, and what you have will be Mine."

He traded your guilt for glory!

You had nothing but debits, and He has nothing but credits. You had nothing but poverty, and He is all wealth. You had nothing but sickness, and He is all health. You had nothing but sin, and He is absolutely holy.

What a glorious exchange!

Your Heavenly Advocate

The devil condemns; the Holy Spirit convicts. Satan accuses you before God day and night. The devil says, you're guilty; you're a human being; you're in an earth suit; you were born of a woman, and sin courses through your veins.

"Guilty, God, he's guilty!"

Jesus replies, "Make your best case, prosecuting attorney. I am the Advocate, the attorney for the defense. Accuse him all you want. In fact, you are right; he is guilty. But there's one problem in this courtroom. You are the prosecuting attorney; and I am the attorney for the defense, the Advocate for the accused. The problem you have is that the Judge is totally partial to Me, and He hates you."

"That makes no difference," says the prosecuting attorney. "This man is guilty as charged. You have to be equitable, and this man is guilty. The price must be paid."

"That's right," says the Father. "My judgments are according to truth. This man is guilty as charged. The price must be paid. Yes, Mr. Defense Attorney, you have something to show Me?"

"Uh-huh, Exhibit A." The defense attorney brings into the courtroom an object which is protected by angel wings that are outstretched over it. He rolls the object into the presence of the Judge.

The Judge questions, "What is staining that beautiful seat? It seems a red, crimson stain is ruining that seat."

"Silence in the courtroom. Exhibit A has something to say."

"Speak on," says the Father.

"Speak on," says the attorney for the accused, as He takes His seat.

"Mercy, mercy; the price is paid in full," is the reply.

The Bible says in the book of Hebrews that the blood on the mercy seat speaks better things than that of Abel, for the blood of Abel cried out, "guilt and vengeance;" but the blood on the mercy seat in the eternal courtroom of God's justice speaks for mercy.

"And to Jesus the mediator of the new covenant, and to the blood of sprinkling, that speaketh better things than that of Abel."

Hebrews 12:24

Now the Judge pronounces the sentence.

"My judgments are according to truth. I have heard the arguments from the prosecution and from the defense. In My solemn wisdom, the defendant is guilty as charged."

Immediately, the devil jumps up and wants to clamp chains on your wrist and lead you away captive. But just before he drags you out of the courtroom, the Father says, "Wait just a minute. I have yet to pass the sentence. Guilty, yes; and here's the sentence: I hold you blameless. The price is paid in full. Guilty, but blameless."

That is the reason repentance is repentance, not an excuse. You cannot make an excuse – you are standing there with the evidence of your guilt. What are you going to say?

We are sinners, everyone, with sin's curse coursing through our bloodstream.

> **"For all have sinned, and come short of the glory of God."**
>
> **Romans 3:23**

This disease called "sin" is acquired, universal in its scope. It does not care if you are black or white, Greek or Jew, tall or short, skinny or stout, affluent or in poverty. It is a universal curse, and it needs a universal cure. From Calvary's crimson red cross, the Son of God cried, "Blameless."

Our iniquity was laid upon Him, and He translated us out of the kingdom of darkness and put us into the kingdom of light.

Though your sins be red as scarlet, through Him they shall be white as snow. He paid the price. You are guilty, but you are free; condemned to death, but you live.

You cannot do enough works, because you are guilty. Nothing you will ever do can erase the "guilty." If you were not guilty, you would not need mercy or grace or Calvary. But you are guilty from the very moment of Adam's original transgression in the Garden of Eden.

Sin was not present before that transgression. The earth was not created in a state of sinfulness and wretchedness. The earth was created in a state of blessing. But from the moment Adam partook of the fruit of the tree of the knowledge of good and evil, this disease was acquired.

You caught it, you have it; and denial will not make it go away.

I knew a woman who had a little blemish on her face. It began to spread, so she put makeup on to cover it. Her family warned her, "You'd better get that taken care of by a doctor." Not listening to their warnings, she did nothing about it. During the summer months, she would even take a scarf and try to hide the facial sore, denying it was even there. The sore continued to fester until, finally, the woman needed major medical attention to resolve the problem.

In the same way, many in the church today would deny their sin, pretending it is not there until it festers into a major problem. Preachers are crying out, "Warning! You have a condition. You'd better get it taken care of! The wages of this disease is death. The soul with this condition will die – better get it taken care of."

Yet, many continue to deny their sin, hoping it will "just go away." Sticking a little religious makeup on sin will not make it disappear. You do not need a cover-up; you need a cure!

Thank God For Mercy

When God looks at me, He says, "You are guilty, but I hold you blameless."

I do not want justice. Instead, I cry, "Lord, give me mercy, because I'm guilty. Do not let the devil – the prosecuting attorney – drag me into hell to spend eternity. Though I deserve it, give me mercy, clemency. Give me a reprieve. I am sentenced to death; but if You will send down the order, they will take me off death row and put me on the street again."

Jesus took you and me off of death row and put us on the street again. We were guilty as charged, but He held us blameless.

> **"They that observe lying vanities** [and say they are not guilty] **forsake their own mercy."**
>
> **Jonah 2:8**

That is why it is hard to believe a lie – because the Holy Ghost will begin to convince you of the truth; and you will become convicted and cry out, "I'm guilty."

Condemnation accuses unjustly. We do not receive unjust condemnation. We do receive the conviction of the Holy Ghost. If there is anything we need in our churches today, it is the moving, wooing, drawing power of the Holy Ghost to convict us of our sin and convince us of righteousness.

I am only held blameless by the acceptance of that blood. I cannot pay the price. The Judge says, "Will you accept or reject Jesus' payment for your guilt?" Every human being on the face of the earth is already held blameless in the eyes of God. That is why He weeps over us. He sees us in the place of corruption and weeps, because He is in the presence of Calvary.

God says, "I can't make you accept this price; but, if you will, I'll hold you blameless."

If I reject that price, I'm guilty.

The question today is: What will you do? Do not try to mask your sin – you are guilty of rejecting God, guilty because you were born into this earth.

Guilty.

The sentence of death for your guilt hangs over your head; but, if you will believe the truth, you can be free. If you will accept the price paid, you can be free and held blameless. If you have been covering over the sin problem with religion, good works, or self-sufficiency, you are wasting your time. If you have been trying to dull the screaming of the sin monster by drowning it in alcohol, it will not work. If you have been trying to silence it with drugs, then you have believed a lie. None of these sins will satisfy you. But if you cry out for mercy, mercy will rewrite your life, and you will walk out of that courtroom saying, "Amazing grace! How sweet the sound that saved a wretch like me! I once was lost, but now am found; was blind, but now I see."[3]

What a marvelous, miracle reality!

Walking Outside of Mercy

Never become so righteous you forget where you came from. Be humbled in the presence of God. You have no excuse, but you have repentance. You know what you have done, but you know who He is and what He has done for you. There is joy in your salvation when you recognize you are guilty but held blameless. Conviction causes you to recognize you are guilty.

Do not observe a lying vanity that says you are okay when you know you are not. If you do so, you forsake mercy. Some of you are walking outside of mercy; you have unforgiveness, bitterness, and strife in your heart; you have stolen other people's happiness.

There is idolatry in your life. Your job is your god or your family is your god, not God Himself. You care more about getting your children to their baseball game on Wednesday night than you do about getting yourself to a prayer meeting.

It must stop; it just has to stop!

Some of you give no mercy; therefore, you get no mercy. You sit on the seat of God's judgment, and you judge; you criticize.

You lie. You told the IRS you made $50,000, because you hid that $5,000 – you know you did. You have stolen tithes and offerings. You have made excuses.

You do not need excuses; you are guilty. Excuses will not help you. You need mercy.

"Pastor Parsley, you don't know what I've done," you protest.

Well, I do know this – what you have done does not matter, because God has enough mercy for you! There are not enough excuses, but there is enough mercy.

Is your relationship with God up to date? If it isn't, you need to cry out for mercy. One step away from what you know is truth is one step too many. Repent and turn around. You need mercy.

You Cannot Do It

Here is the good news!

> **"And the very God of peace sanctify you wholly; and I pray God your whole spirit and soul and body be preserved blameless unto the coming of our Lord Jesus Christ."**
>
> **1 Thessalonians 5:23**

And verse 24 says, **"Faithful is he that calleth you, who also will do it."**

Do what?

Keep you!

You cannot do it by yourself. Every time temptation comes along, you say, "I'm not going to yield to it." You try in yourself; and try as you might, you still fail.

You need to realize you cannot do it. It takes Jesus on the inside of you to resist temptation. You have to move out of the way and say, "Live through me, Holy Ghost, right now; in the face of temptation, live."

But if you try on your own, you will not have the power to resist; and you will fail.

Because we are human beings, the easiest thing for us to do is to slowly move out of conviction and slip into condemnation. We want to punish ourselves; if we punish ourselves we forsake mercy.

Jesus already took your punishment. You are not destined to be punished. God has declared you guilty, but blameless.

Endnotes

[1] Walter B. Knight, *Knight's Master Book of New Illustrations* (Grand Rapids: Eerdman's Printing Company, 1956), p. 286.

[2] *Ibid.,* pp. 286, 287.

[3] *The United Methodist Hymnal* (Nashville: The United Methodist Publishing House, 1989), p. 378

Your Salvation Tool Kit

Here Are the Tools, the Spiritual Hammer and Nails, You Need to Biblically Repair the Salvation Plank in Your Life.

Salvation is a term that means much more than forgiveness of sin. The word most often translated salvation also carries the ideas of preservation, soundness, deliverance, health, and peace. Salvation actually contains anything you need from the Lord. However, salvation certainly includes the forgiveness of sin, which is probably the most dramatic individual benefit a person receives as a result of making Jesus Christ his Lord and Savior. In this lesson we will examine salvation in detail.

I.   Three Principles Involved in Salvation

Repentance

Repentance is to turn around, turn away from, to change the mind followed by a change in behavior.

You must turn away from sin. Sin is more than just individual acts of unrighteousness (sins), even though they are involved. Sin is the old nature – the nature of the devil; separated from God.

John 8:44 Ye are of your father the devil, and the lusts of your father ye will do. He was a murderer from the beginning, and abode not in the truth, because there is no truth in him. When he speaketh a lie, he speaketh of his own: for he is a liar, and the father of it.

Matthew 6:24 No man can serve two masters: for either he will hate the one, and love the other; or else he will hold to the one, and despise the other. Ye cannot serve God and mammon.

Believing Something

Ephesians 2:8 For by grace are ye saved through faith; and that not of yourselves: it is the gift of God:

v. 9 Not of works, lest any man should boast.

What do you believe? That God raised Jesus from the dead – that Jesus is alive! No other religion claims to have a living Savior – they are all dead!

The resurrection is the keystone of Biblical Christianity. It was the central theme of the preaching of the New Testament church.

1 Corinthians 15:12 Now if Christ be preached that he rose from the dead, how say some among you that there is no resurrection of the dead?

v. 13 But if there be no resurrection of the dead, then is Christ not risen:

v. 14 And if Christ be not risen, then is our preaching vain, and your faith is also vain.

v. 15 Yea, and we are found false witnesses of God; because we have testified of God that he raised up Christ: whom he raised not up, if so be that the dead rise not.

v. 16 For if the dead rise not, then is not Christ raised:

v. 17 And if Christ be not raised, your faith is vain; ye are yet in your sins.

v. 18 Then they also which are fallen asleep in Christ are perished.

v. 19 If in this life only we have hope in Christ, we are of all men most miserable.

v. 20 But now is Christ risen from the dead, and become the firstfruits of them that slept.

v. 21 For since by man came death, by man came also the resurrection of the dead.

v. 22 For as in Adam all die, even so in Christ shall all be made alive.

Acts 10:39 And we are witnesses of all things which he did both in the land of the Jews, and in Jerusalem; whom they slew and hanged on a tree:

v. 40 Him God raised up the third day, and shewed him openly.

Acts 17:2 And Paul, as his manner was, went in unto them, and three sabbath days reasoned with them out of the scriptures,

v. 3   Opening and alleging, that Christ must needs have suffered, and risen again from the dead; and that this Jesus, whom I preach unto you, is Christ.

Romans 1:3 Concerning his Son Jesus Christ our Lord, which was made of the seed of David according to the flesh;

v. 4   And declared to be the Son of God with power, according to the spirit of holiness, by the resurrection from the dead.

2 Corinthians 4:14 Knowing that he which raised up the Lord Jesus shall raise up us also by Jesus, and shall present us with you.

Revelation 1:18 I am he that liveth, and was dead; and, behold, I am alive for evermore, Amen; and have the keys of hell and of death.

Saying Something

Romans 10:9 That if thou shalt confess with thy mouth the Lord Jesus, and shalt believe in thine heart that God hath raised him from the dead, thou shalt be saved.

v. 10   For with the heart man believeth unto righteousness; and with the mouth confession is made unto salvation.

Matthew 12:34 ...for out of the abundance of the heart, the mouth speaketh.

Proverbs 18:21 Death and life are in the power of the tongue...

Mark 11:22 And Jesus answering saith unto them, Have faith in God.

v. 23 For verily I say unto you, That whosoever shall say unto this mountain, Be thou removed, and be thou cast into the sea; and shall not doubt in his heart, but shall believe that those things which he saith shall come to pass; he shall have whatsoever he saith.

v. 24 Therefore I say unto you, What things soever ye desire, when ye pray, believe that ye receive them, and ye shall have them.

II.   What God Has Done for You

Substitution

Substitution is when one person or thing is put in or takes the place of another person or thing.

Matthew 20:28 Even as the Son of man came not to be ministered unto, but to minister, and to give his life a ransom for many.

John 1:29 The next day John seeth Jesus coming unto him, and saith, Behold the Lamb of God, which taketh away the sin of the world.

Redemption

Redemption is to purchase, buy back from, return to the original state of affairs.

1 Corinthians 6:19 What? know ye not that your body is the temple of the Holy Ghost which is in you, which ye have of God, and ye are not your own?

v. 20 For ye are bought with a price: therefore glorify God in your body, and in your spirit, which are God's.

Galatians 3:13 Christ hath redeemed us from the curse of the law, being made a curse for us: for it is written, Cursed is every one that hangeth on a tree.

Hebrews 9:18 Whereupon neither the first testament was dedicated without blood.

v. 19. For when Moses had spoken every precept to all the people according to the law, he took the blood of calves and of goats, with water, and scarlet wool, and hyssop, and sprinkled both the book, and all the people,

v. 20 Saying, This is the blood of the testament which God hath enjoined unto you.

v. 21 Moreover he sprinkled with blood both the tabernacle, and all the vessels of the ministry.

v. 22 And almost all things are by the law purged with blood; and without shedding of blood is no remission.

Hebrews 10:1 For the law having a shadow of good things to come, and not the very image of the things, can never with those sacrifices which they offered year by year continually make the comers thereunto perfect.

v. 2 For then would they not have ceased to be offered? because that the worshippers once purged should have had no more conscience of sins.

v. 3 But in those sacrifices there is a remembrance again made of sins every year.

v. 4 For it is not possible that the blood of bulls and of goats should take away sins.

Hebrews 9:13 For if the blood of bulls and of goats, and the ashes of an heifer sprinkling the unclean, sanctifieth to the purifying of the flesh:

v. 14 How much more shall the blood of Christ, who through the eternal Spirit offered himself without spot to God, purge your conscience from dead works to serve the living God?

v. 15 And for this cause he is the mediator of the new testament, that by means of death, for the redemption of the transgressions that were under the first testament, they which are called might receive the promise of eternal inheritance.

Hebrews 9:23 It was therefore necessary that the patterns of things in the heavens should be purified with these; but the heavenly things themselves with better sacrifices than these.

v. 24 For Christ is not entered into the holy places made with hands, which are the figures of the true; but into heaven itself, now to appear in the presence of God for us:

v. 25 Nor yet that he should offer himself often, as the high priest entereth into the holy place every year with blood of others;

v. 26 For then must he often have suffered since the foundation of the world: but now once in the end of the world hath he appeared to put away sin by the sacrifice of himself.

v. 27 And as it is appointed unto men once to die, but after this the judgment:

v. 28 So Christ was once offered to bear the sins of many; and unto them that look for him shall he appear the second time without sin unto salvation.

Propitiation

Propitiation is satisfaction of God's righteous demands.

Romans 3:25 Whom God hath set forth to be a propitiation through faith in his blood, to declare his righteousness for the remission of sins that are past, through the forbearance of God.

Psalm 89:34 My covenant will I not break, nor alter the thing that is gone out of my lips.

Romans 3:26 To declare, I say, at this time his righteousness: that he might be just, and the justifier of him which believeth in Jesus.

Romans 3:28 Therefore we conclude that a man is justified by faith without the deeds of the law.

Romans 11:32 For God hath concluded them all in unbelief, that he might have mercy upon all.

Reconciliation

Reconciliation is to exchange from hatred to friendship – an act of God which enables man to fellowship with Him.

2 Corinthians 5:18 And all things are of God, who hath reconciled us to himself by Jesus Christ, and hath given to us the ministry of reconciliation;

v. 19 To wit, that God was in Christ, reconciling the world unto himself, not imputing their trespasses unto them; and hath committed unto us the word of reconciliation.

Forgiveness

Forgiveness is to send forth, to send away from – also involves forgetting about it.

Hebrews 10:17 And their sins and iniquities will I remember no more.

Justification

Justification is declaration of righteousness.

Romans 3:26 To declare, I say, at this time his righteousness: that he might be just, and the justifier of him which believeth in Jesus.

1 Corinthians 6:11 And such were some of you: but ye are washed, but ye are sanctified, but ye are justified in the name of the Lord Jesus, and by the Spirit of our God.

Righteousness

Righteousness is right standing with God – no sense of guilt, shame, or condemnation.

Hebrews 10:19 Having therefore, brethren, boldness to enter into the holiest by the blood of Jesus,

v. 20 By a new and living way, which he hath consecrated for us, through the veil, that is to say, his flesh;

v. 21 And having an high priest over the house of God;

v. 22 Let us draw near with a true heart in full assurance of faith, having our hearts sprinkled from an evil conscience, and our bodies washed with pure water.

Sanctification

Sanctification is being set apart for a holy purpose.

1 Corinthians 6:11 And such were some of you: but ye are washed, but ye are sanctified, but ye are justified in the name of the Lord Jesus, and by the Spirit of our God.

Hebrews 10:10 By the which will we are sanctified through the offering of the body of Jesus Christ once for all.

Life

Life is union with God.

John 3:15 That whosoever believeth in him should not perish, but have eternal life.

v. 16 For God so loved the world, that he gave his only begotten Son, that whosoever believeth in him should not perish, but have everlasting life.

v. 17 For God sent not his Son into the world to condemn the world; but that the world through him might be saved.

III. What Happens to You Inside

Before and After Salvation

Ephesians 2:2 Wherein in time past ye walked according to the course of this world, according to the prince of the power of the air, the spirit that now worketh in the children of disobedience:

v. 3 Among whom also we all had our conversation in times past in the lusts of our flesh, fulfilling the desires of the flesh and of the mind; and were by nature the children of wrath, even as others.

Ephesians 4:22 That ye put off concerning the former conversation the old man, which is corrupt according to the deceitful lusts.

Ephesians 2:12 That at that time ye were without Christ, being aliens from the commonwealth of Israel, and strangers from the covenants of promise, having no hope, and without God in the world.

Colossians 2:13 And you, being dead in your sins and the uncircumcision of your flesh, hath he quickened together with him, having forgiven you all trespasses.

Ephesians 2:13 But now in Christ Jesus ye who sometimes were far off are made nigh by the blood of Christ.

2 Corinthians 6:14 Be ye not unequally yoked together with unbelievers: for what fellowship hath righteousness with unrighteousness? and what communion hath light with darkness?

v. 15 And what concord hath Christ with Belial? or what part hath he that believeth with an infidel?

v. 16 And what agreement hath the temple of God with idols? for ye are the temple of the living God; as God hath said, I will dwell in them, and walk in them; and I will be their God, and they shall be my people.

Different Terms Used to Describe the Same Thing

Romans 10:10 For with the heart man believeth unto righteousness; and with the mouth confession is made unto <u>salvation</u>.

John 3:3 Jesus answered and said unto him, Verily, verily, I say unto thee, Except a man be <u>born again</u>, he cannot see the kingdom of God.

Some Changes That Take Place

2 Corinthians 5:17 Therefore if any man be in Christ, he is a new creature: old things are passed away; behold, all things are become new.

Ezekiel 36:26 A new heart also will I give you, and a new spirit will I put within you: and I will take away the stony heart out of your flesh, and I will give you an heart of flesh.

Romans 10:9 That if thou shalt confess with thy mouth the Lord Jesus, and shalt believe in thine heart that God hath raised him from the dead, thou shalt be saved.

v. 10 For with the heart man believeth unto righteousness; and with the mouth confession is made unto salvation.

John 5:24 Verily, verily, I say unto you, He that heareth my word, and believeth on him that sent me, hath everlasting life, and shall not come into condemnation; but is passed from death unto life.

1 John 3:14 We know that we have passed from death unto life, because we love the brethren. He that loveth not his brother abideth in death.

Ephesians 2:4 But God, who is rich in mercy, for his great love wherewith he loved us,

v. 5 Even when we were dead in sins, hath quickened us together with Christ, (by grace ye are saved;)

v. 6 And hath raised us up together, and made us sit together in heavenly places in Christ Jesus.

Ephesians 1:7 In whom we have redemption through his blood, the forgiveness of sins, according to the riches of his grace.

Romans 3:25 Whom God hath set forth to be a propitiation through faith in his blood, to declare his righteousness for the remission of sins that are past, through the forbearance of God;

v. 26 To declare, I say, at this time his righteousness: that he might be just, and the justifier of him which believeth in Jesus.

John 1:12 But as many as received him, to them gave he power to become the sons of God, even to them that believe on his name.

1 Corinthians 12:13 For by one Spirit are we all baptized into one body, whether we be Jews or Gentiles, whether we be bond or free; and have been all made to drink into one Spirit.

IV. The Transformation Continues

Our Spirit Is New

2 Corinthians 5:17 Therefore if any man be in Christ, he is a new creature: old things are passed away; behold, all things are become new.

Renewing Our Mind

Romans 12:2 And be not conformed to this world: but be ye transformed by the renewing of your mind, that ye may prove what is that good, and acceptable, and perfect, will of God.

Bringing Our Body Under Subjection

1 Corinthians 9:27 But I keep under my body, and bring it into subjection: lest that by any means, when I have preached to others, I myself should be a castaway.

God Is Interested In Our Total Being

1 Thessalonians 5:23 And the very God of peace sanctify you wholly; and I pray God your whole spirit and soul and body be preserved blameless unto the coming of our Lord Jesus Christ.

We Are Being Changed

2 Corinthians 3:18 But we all, with open face beholding as in a glass the glory of the Lord, are changed into the same image from glory to glory, even as by the Spirit of the Lord.

Salvation has been purchased by the blood of Jesus Christ so we can have eternal life and fellowship with God. The benefits of salvation touch every conceivable area of our lives. The more we find out about the subject of salvation, the more we realize the goodness, mercy, and ultimate wisdom of our loving Heavenly Father.

PLANK THREE

_____

Restoring Freedom to the
Body of Christ

_____

PLANK THREE

Restoring Freedom to the Body of Christ

The Power of Praise

When the armies of Napoleon swept over Europe, one of his generals made a surprising attack on the little town of Feldkirch, on the Austrian border. As Napoleon's formidable army maneuvered on the heights above Feldkirch, a council of its citizens was hastily summoned to decide whether to surrender or attempt a defense.

In this assembly the venerable dean of the church arose to declare: "This is Easter Day. We have been counting on our own strength, and that will fail. This is the day of our Lord's resurrecttion. Let us ring the bells and have services as usual, and leave the matter in God's hands. We know only our weakness and not the power of God."

The council accepted his plan, and in a few minutes the church belfry chimed the joyous bells announcing the Savior's resurrection.

The enemy, hearing the sudden peal, concluded that the Austrian army had arrived during the night, broke up camp, and before the Easter bells had ceased, the danger had been lifted.

— Lutheran Hour[1]

WHO: Who can cast out demons? Jesus said in Mark 16:17 that it would be done by **"them that believe."** The example in Acts 19 of Sceva's sons shows that demons don't obey non-believers.

Examples of successful exorcisms in the Bible range from the sinless Jesus to an ex-murderer of believers, Paul (Acts 16:18). If someone foolishly wants to put aside the Bible and take as their model today's popular films and books on the occult, then they are going to conclude that exorcism is complex and done by the select few.

However, the Bible says the opposite:

WHAT: What tools do we need? According to Ephesians 6:17 and Mark 11:23, the only tool necessary is your own faith and the Word of God – the "sword of the Spirit."

WHEN: When do we exorcise demons? After you pray – just you and the Lord – tell the thing to go. Invoke the authority of Jesus Christ.

If the evil thing wants to chat, quote Scripture at it – particularly "power verses" such as Colossians 1:16, Ephesians 1:21, Colossians 2:10,15, Romans 8:37-39, and Ephesians 6:12.

Remember that when Jesus Christ commanded Satan to leave, the devil obeyed. Satan had to bow to the greater authority.

WHERE: Where should demons be cast out? I cast out demons in stadiums filled with thousands, and in my office with a few believers gathered around the afflicted person. Examples in the Bible say it happened in public or in a setting with a few people. Do not try exorcism, however, on Satan's turf, such as in a satanic coven's meeting or in a pagan temple.

WHY: Why should we prepare ourselves? Jesus emphasized to the disciples the extreme importance of prayer and fasting in Matthew 17:21. It is so important.

Also, I personally have seen the effectiveness of memorizing scriptures. You need to be armed with God's Word to show the demon your authority. Memorized promises also are good for you – to build up your own faith and confidence that you do, indeed, have divine authority to be doing this sort of thing.

— Dr. Lester Sumrall[2]

Devil, Put It Back!

An American university, which has one of the largest student body campuses in the world, found in a recent survey that many of the males attending the university admitted that at some time in their lives they had experienced some form of homosexual activity.

Many teenage girls have already had sex by the time they reach age thirteen! It is little wonder, then, that teenage pregnancies continue to escalate; and the world now needs to be delivered from a little virus that holds entire continents at bay, a virus that is the greatest epidemic ever to sweep the North American continent, a virus that has already robbed this nation of more men than did the entire Vietnam War.

Nations are spending millions of dollars to try and find a cure for this little virus; yet, AIDS continues to escalate at an alarming rate.

Demon activity is rampant.

The devil is attacking our youth, and he is attacking our marriages. Infidelity in America is at its highest. It is little wonder, then, that in 2002 (the latest date with statistics available) 34 percent of all American newborns lived with a never-married parent.[3]

The devil is stealing our morality and is offering us the pathetic substitutes of temporary earthly pleasures.

We are a nation of alcoholics and consume more hard liquor than any nation on the face of this earth. When you drive down the road, you always run the risk of a car or a truck coming across the center line to snuff out your life – vehicles driven by intoxicated drivers.

America needs to be delivered from its addictions.

From alcohol.

Drugs.

Pornography.

Too much television.

The devil is killing our kids and destroying our unborn babies at record rates.

Demon activity permeates our world.

War stories of soldiers treating innocent children cruelly have even been reported.

How much more will we allow the devil to take?

Who is going to come forward and declare, in the name of Jesus, that it is time for deliverance? It is time to be free of bondage!

Who is going to demand that the devil get out of the satanic worship in our cities, the abortion clinics in our suburbs, and the pornographic movies in our video rental locations?

Who is going to serve notice on Satan that his time is over to infect our population with cancer, heart disease, and other sicknesses?

Who is going to tell him to stop splitting our families?

Satan is not going to relinquish his stranglehold just because it is the right thing to do. He is not going to loose his death grip because you think he should. He is not going to release this nation from crack addiction or homosexual perversion just because you wish he would.

The devil has stolen the plank of freedom from our lives and is now holding us in bondage. Now is the time for the Body of Christ to experience deliverance.

It is time to get serious, to get delivered, and to restore the freedom plank the devil has stolen from the Body of Christ.

Enough Is Enough!

The devil is a trespasser and a thief.

He has no right of dominion.

He did not get into this world the right way to have dominion.

But freedom is never granted voluntarily by the oppressor. It must be demanded by the oppressed. Somebody has to stand up, put their foot down, put their finger under the nose of satanic oppression, and say once and for all, "Enough is enough."

In Genesis, God gave dominion to Adam's race. Through Adam's sin, Satan stole dominion of this planet. Jesus came to take it back. It is our job to see to it that Satan puts it back and leaves it alone.

Deliverance produces freedom – which belongs to the Body of Christ. This plank must be restored to God's bridge of grace!

In John 10, Jesus said that He came through the door of human birth and that anyone who comes in any other way is a thief and a robber. To have the right dominion on planet earth, one must have been born through a woman – Adam's dominion – and born again spiritually – Jesus' dominion.

Jesus told Nicodemus it was necessary to be born of water (natural birth) and of the Spirit (salvation). Satan has neither qualification.

The devil has no legal authority on this earth. When God formed man of the dust of the ground, He gave him earthly authority. God breathed into his nostrils the breath of life, and man became a living soul.

When the demon spirit of Gadera began to cry out when Jesus cast it out, it did not say, "Thou Son of man." It said, **"...thou Son of the most high God? I adjure thee by God, that thou torment me not" (Mark 5:7).**

Did the demon go to preaching for God?

No, that is not what happened.

It knew that as the Son of God, He was a Spirit being. As long as He was a Spirit being, he had no authority on the face of the earth. But Jesus came not only as the Son of God, but as the Son of man. He said, "Devil, shut up; and come out of him."

And he had to come out.

The world "adjure" means literally, I bind you. What the demon of Gadera was saying was, "Jesus, I bind You by the most high God." That is astonishing – demons trying to bind Jesus! If all it said was true, then it would have been within its rights.

Jesus, however, was not operating as the Son of God (a Spirit being); He was operating as a Spirit-filled man. Jesus limited Himself to His humanity and demonstrated the Holy Spirit to show that we all have the same Holy Spirit available to us. That is why He

125

said, **"...He that believeth on me, the works that I do shall he do also..." (John 14:12).**

If Jesus had operated as "God-in-disguise," as the Son of God, then there would have been no way we could imitate Him. Thank God Jesus operated in the same Holy Ghost available to us. We can say with Jesus, **"The Spirit of the Lord is upon me, because he hath anointed me...to preach deliverance..." (Luke 4:18).**

That is the reason we clap our hands in praise and worship. When we do, we show our earthly authority – the sound of flesh on flesh. Spirits cannot do that because they have no fleshly body. As long as we are in an earth suit, we have authority.

Because we are born again, we have the anointing, the authority, to drive the works of hell out of our lives and out of the lives of others.

"Let him that stole steal no more..." (Ephesians 4:28).

Proverbs 6:31 says of a thief, **"If he be found, he shall restore sevenfold; he shall give all the substance of his house."**

Joel 2:25 promises that God will **"Restore to you the years that the locust hath eaten..."**

God is saying, "I'm going to give back to you what the devil has stolen. Not only am I going to give it back, I'm going to give it back seven times stronger than it's ever been on the face of this earth."

I appreciate the Whitefield revival, the Lutheran revival, and the Wesleyan revival. I thank God for the healing revival, the Charismatic renewal, and the Word of Faith renewal.

But I have news for you. I have my eyes set on something greater! I believe the greatest revival that has ever slapped the sides of the earth is ready to spout over the sapphire sill of heaven's gate and cover the earth like the waters cover the sea.

We serve an omnipotent God.

"Omni" means – "without restriction"[4] – many, and "potent" means potential.[5] There is potential in God that is yet to be seen on the face of the earth. There is a revival coming out of the heart of God that is going to literally shake kingdoms, and entire nations are going to be born in a day. We are the people of the decade of dominion, a people of destiny.

There is a revival coming to the face of the earth unlike any other God has ever sent forth. I see a time when hospitals are going to be emptied, when we are going to have church twenty-four hours a day. I see a time when every cripple will walk out of their wheelchair, when all the deaf will begin to hear, when every mute will begin to speak. I believe we are going to see a move of God where blind eyes being opened is going to be as commonplace as a Sunday school picnic.

In Mark 9, we read the story of the little boy tormented by an evil spirit which would throw him into the fire and into the water. His father took the boy to Jesus' disciples. They could not do anything for him.

When the father saw Jesus, he went to Him and said, "Lord, have mercy on us. My little boy throws himself in the fire and foams at the mouth. I took him to your disciples, and they could not help him."

I love the answer Jesus gave to the man: **"...bring him unto me" (Mark 9:19)**, and then He healed him.

In Luke 4, Peter's mother-in-law was taken with a great fever, so they called on Jesus. The Bible says **"...he stood over her..." (v. 39)**.

God is standing over you today. He is standing between you and the forces of darkness that would try to assail you and stop you.

God is standing between you and sickness, disease, pain, infirmity, malady, and malfunction.

And Jesus never "counseled" out a devil. He confronted them and cast them out! He is not just standing there silently. The Bible says that when Jesus stood over her, He **"...rebuked the fever; and it left her: and immediately she arose and ministered unto them" (Luke 4:39)**. "Rebuke" means He pointed His finger at the devil and said, "Stop it! That's enough!"

We need to tell the devil, "Stop it! That's enough! You have stolen enough power out of the church. You have stolen enough of the basic tenets of faith, so that people can no longer get across the bridge of grace."

We need deliverance, but we cannot get across the bridge.

We must become repairers of the breach, restorers of paths to dwell in. We must command the devil to get his hands off the basic beliefs of gospel truth and allow revival to sweep across the world like a wildfire of the glory and majesty of Almighty God.

Command the Devil, "Leave me alone!"

My sister, Debbie, needed to be delivered; the devil was trying to kill her. During the time we sought God as a family for her deliverance, we stood on Hebrews 11:6.

> **"But without faith it is impossible to please him; for he that cometh to God must believe that he is, and that he is a rewarder of them that diligently seek him."**

Debbie was on nearly 40 prescribed medications a day. The doctors told us, "We're going to give her all the vials and needles of Demerol she can stand." We brought her medicine home in boxes. The doctors told us, "She has three months maximum to live."

But the Parsley household did not accept the doctor's declaration of doom.

Instead, we looked to God for her deliverance.

In 1979, we drove to Indianapolis, Indiana, for a week to go into intensive deliverance prayer with Norvel Hayes.

I will let Norvel tell you what happened.

"I prayed for Debbie for about five days. On Friday night, the fifth night, the Word of the Lord came to me saying, 'Put your arms around her, hold her close to you, and command that thing to loose her.'

"Now, I knew that without faith it is impossible to please God, and I knew that God was Debbie's rewarder – that she did not have to stay in that condition for the rest of her life. For five days I had prayed, and for five days she never said a word – just stood there and stared at me. Didn't even flinch. I would say, 'In Jesus' name, you devil that's trying to wreck this girl's life, come out of her,' and she would not move.

"The only way you can ever break the devil's power over a human being is to show the devil, in Jesus' name, that you're stronger than him. You can't just tell him; you must show him!

"So I refused to be discouraged by her blank stares. I knew the devil was powerful in her; he did not want to turn her loose and let her go. He wanted to kill her.

"Faith people don't give up. That Friday night I put my arms around Debbie, pulled her close to me, and refused to let go. I stood in front of the congregation with Debbie in my arms for almost three hours. I told the devil, 'You're not going to have this girl's mind. I'm not going to let you have it; in Jesus' name, you have to obey me.'

"Well, that was the first time the devil ever came right into a service where I was at and tried to pull somebody out of my arms. Right there in that church, he tried to pull her out of my arms.

"'You can't have her,' I told him. She stuck her nails in my back, and I was hurting so bad I could hardly stand it. The devil was trying to suck her out of my arms. If I could have seen in the spirit world, I know I would have seen big demons holding her legs and pulling her.

"Finally, Debbie opened her mouth and said, 'Leave me alone! I'm not going with you! These people love me, and I'm not going with you. You've done horrible things to me, and I'm not going with you.'

"Then she stuck her nails in my back and held onto me. One of her legs was being pulled straight out by an invisible force. I tried to push it down, but I couldn't. I told four men standing near me, 'Push down her leg'; but the power of four men pushing against that ninety-two pound girl, putting their weight on her so much that they lifted themselves off the ground, could not push that leg down. That little teenager's leg stuck straight out, and four men couldn't push it down. During all of this, Debbie kept saying, 'Leave me alone. I'm not going with you!'

"While all of this was going on, God's words kept ringing in my spirit – 'I am the rewarder of them that diligently seek me.' You have to seek Him by faith. Sheer faith. Bold faith. For almost three hours that night, we showed the devil we were not going to give up, that we were going to bug him until he just gave up – and he finally did. God delivered Debbie that night!"

You have spent your last defeated day, your last blue Monday! Never again will you say, "I just don't know what to do." Greater is the God in you than any demon or devil! God's Word, which knows no boundaries, will set you free, just as it set Debbie free. If the devil does not jump the first time you tell him, then keep telling him. Keep being diligent, and God will honor your prayers, and the devil must flee.

The Parsley family did not give up.

Norvel Hayes did not give up.

And after five days, Debbie declared to the devil with her own words, "Leave me alone."

Finally, the devil gave up and left.

Grace: God's Power to Deliver!

Faith is by grace, not something you obtain or produce through works. There are no set formulas to learn to muster faith.

> **"Therefore it is of faith, that it might be by grace..."**
>
> **Romans 4:16**

Faith is by grace; grace is the gift before faith. Faith is not something you must work to conjure up in your life. Grace provided the faith through which you were saved.

For too many years, Christians have accepted a gospel of humanism that says we have to work for faith. The Bible says faith comes through grace – the unmerited favor of God which produces the availability of God's power to deliver you, to give you the freedom to move mountains.

Many Christians operate in a low degree of faith because they think they have to work for it.

But faith is by grace.

> **"For by grace are ye saved through faith; and that not of yourselves; it is the gift of God: Not of works, lest any man should boast."**
>
> **Ephesians 2:8-9**

Everything you receive in this kingdom, you are going to receive by grace. Faith in God can bring victory in every area of your life, and it comes by grace.

Before you had any faith, there was grace; grace came and gave you faith. God has not stopped giving faith – He is still imparting faith to you. That is the reason your spirit man on the inside of you is always full of faith.

The Spirit Man Believes

It is not your spirit man that is full of doubt and unbelief; it is your soul – your mind, your will, and your emotions. Your spirit man will believe. When you hear somebody preach under the anointing or you read something in the Word, something on the inside of you just says, "Yes! Yes! Yes!"

Your spirit man believes whatever God says. Your spirit man will believe Jonah was swallowed up by a minnow if that is what God says. Your spirit man can take your mind's limits off of God.

But then your mental reasoning comes along and says, "No, that just isn't possible!"

Your spirit man will always believe God. Your spirit is inundated with grace; and grace brings, as a gift, faith. Grace says, "You don't have enough faith to get it? That's all right. Here's grace. I'll give you faith to get it."

God gave you grace, and you were saved by that gift of faith that came by grace. When your faith has gone to its limit, God says, "That's all right; there's still grace."

When your faith cannot produce what you need, just cry out for mercy.

We have had this idea that God abandons us at the limits of our faith. We draw that line. We say, "Right there; that's where I can believe." If all we are going to get in this end-time revival is what some poor pitiful human being can believe for, God help us all!

Remember, you are just a hunk of flesh. You may fall apart because you feel your faith falls short of some imaginary mark your mind creates. Well, quit complaining! God is not limited by your flesh.

I am not telling you to give up on your faith; I am just telling you not to limit God! Never limit His actions by anything that has to do with you.

Did you know God has more faith in you than you do in yourself?

At the Last Supper, Jesus tells Peter,

> **"Simon, Simon, behold, Satan hath desired to have you, that he may sift you as wheat:**
>
> **"But I have prayed for thee, that thy faith fail not..."**
>
> **Luke 22:31-32**

That passage actually translates, "Satan hath requisitioned to have you.

I can just imagine what Peter must have been thinking as Jesus spoke these words.

"Wait a minute, Jesus. I left my family business, my wife, and my kids. I gave up a family fortune to come out here with You. I've traveled around with You through these cities and villages. I've been laughed at and thrown in jail."

Have you ever felt that way?

Have you ever felt, "Everybody is always picking on me?" Like the demon hordes of hell lost everybody else's address but yours? Like you are getting your brains beat out by the forces of darkness?

Well, God told Jeremiah, "Cheer up, things are about to get worse." You see, God has more confidence, more faith in you than you have in yourself.

Why?

Because He knows who lives inside of you, and He will never back down to the devil. I think when Satan launches an attack in my life, Jesus must say, "Devil, when you take your best shot at him, just remember, he's washed in the blood of the Lamb. His garments are spotless and he's white as snow. He is fire baptized; and when you touch him, you'll get burned."

God knows you have the power to kick the demon forces of darkness out of your house! God knows the strategies to defeat the devil; He knows the enemy; and He knows you have all the ammunition you need to ward off the enemy's attacks and force him to retreat.

God knows His grace is beyond your faith.

You are going to accomplish things beyond your spiritual ability to believe – through Him. There are going to be things you cannot necessarily "believe God" for that He is going to do – just because He is God.

Grace comes to the limit of our faith and says, "Okay, I'm glad you carried the ball that far; but we are not across the goal line yet. How about if I take a hand-off from you here?"

Ephesians 3:20 says, **"Now unto him that is able to do exceeding abundantly above all that we ask or think..."**

That is beyond your faith.

God can do more than I have faith for.

Some people are shattered when their faith falls short of the mark. They need to remember that God is not limited by their faults or shortcomings.

When you feel that your faith has failed, just throw your hands up and say, "Lord God, I have not been faithful. I didn't believe You to get rid of the cold. I didn't believe You to get rid of the flu. I didn't believe You to get rid of that infection. Now, I have cancer. The doctor has looked at me and said I must die – I have only two weeks to live. God, I don't have time to get myself built up in this weapon of faith, but You have not abandoned me.

"I still believe You are able to deliver me. Your arm is not shortened to deliver me. I believe You can still deliver me, because all things are possible with You. With men it is impossible, but with God all things are possible. I throw myself over on the arms of grace, and I cry out for Your mercy."

I am not telling you to give up on your faith; I am just telling you not to limit God.

> **"Now unto him that is able to do exceeding abundantly above all that we ask or think, according to the power that worketh in us."**
>
> **Ephesians 3:20**

Some things are beyond you, bigger than you, greater than you, higher than your faith, deeper than your believing. In those instances, God is going to say, "I'm going to go beyond human ability, even in faith, and display to this planet that I am God."

We must quit putting God in our little charismatic box and saying, "This is all God can do." God can do anything He wants to do, and He asks no one's permission. It is called "sovereignty" – which means "I am God and you are not."

He says, "When I framed the earth, where were you? And when I sit down at the desk, who stands up at the blackboard? Who instructed Me?"

Part of our problem is that we have been trying to instruct God. "God, You will do this; and You will do it this way. I went to a seminar and they said if I would do one, two, and three, then You would do one, two, and three."

God is not a vending machine, and you do not have the right change.

He is God!

He is going to do what He wants to do, when He wants to do it!

Your faith is not the pinnacle apex of the ability of God. He can do greater things than you can even imagine or hope. He can do greater things than your mind's eye can conceive or your heart can believe, because He's God.

You do not serve a humanistic god of self-help. Your God is not limited by human flesh. Every person God ever used had clay feet. They were thrown into prison, shipwrecked, left for dead; but the kingdom of God kept right on marching, never missing a beat.

God is going to send a revival to this earth that is not bound to the frailty of human flesh. God is going to supersede everything we can believe. We are soon going to see a gully-washing, outpouring, downpour, deluge of Holy Ghost revival that no man's faith is going to trigger or control. God will do it in spite of men and through men.

Stop limiting God by what you believe. Yes, He requires you to believe; but He is not bound by your ability to believe. The God we serve sits on the circumference of the earth. He speaks, and nations crumble. He thinks thoughts, and valleys are made low.

When you begin to think you have grown spiritually to the point where you can accomplish something, that is when God quits working. He will let you fight and struggle until you finally get to the end of yourself; and then, when you are like a little kitty cat wrapped up in yarn, when you cannot do anything but just lay there and meow – then He takes over.

His strength is made complete in your weakness.

Put It Back!

Dr. Lester Sumrall told of the time that a horrible presence came into his room when he was ministering deep in the jungle. All of a sudden, the bed he was in began to shake away from the wall. Now, I do not mean he was shaking in his bed – I mean the bed he was in was shaking! The bed started dancing in the middle of the floor.

Dr. Sumrall said, "I recognized immediately that it was the devil."

Dr. Sumrall sat up in the middle of the bed and said, "Satan, I rebuke you."

The bed immediately stopped shaking. Now, most of us would have been content that the bed stopped shaking. But not Dr. Sumrall. He said, *"Put the bed back where it was,"* and the bed started shaking again and moved back against the wall.

It is time we told the devil to get out and to put back everything he has taken! We do not even want to see the evidence of where he has been.

We need to know how to recognize the devil and then make him leave, taking his mess with him!

A friend of mine was getting ready to go out and minister in gospel music. When he went to climb into his car, he saw the vehicle had a flat tire. So he came back inside and said, "Well, it must not be God's will for me to go."

"No," I replied. "that's the devil."

"What do you mean?" he questioned.

"Well," I said, "if you had gone outside and you had a flat tire, and then the flat tire was healed, that would have been God."

> **"The thief cometh not, but for to steal, and to kill, and to destroy: but I am come that they might have life, and that they might have it more abundantly."**
>
> **John 10:10**

Christians have had such complacency. We think it is such a miracle if the devil just leaves. Well, I have news for you; he is not only going to leave, he is going to take his mess with him!

God wants you not to be satisfied with just making Satan leave. Make him put back what he has taken!

> **"Casting all your care upon him; for he careth for you."**
>
> **1 Peter 5:7**

Who? God cares for you!

If you can ever get that fundamental thought into your spirit, you will learn how to have total victory over the devil. If not, you will be constantly trying to decide if what is going on is the work of the devil.

The first thing you have to get in your spirit is that God is a good God. He cares for you. He said, "I want you to roll all your care over on Me, because I really do care for you."

Sometimes we act like God is up there in heaven with punitive lightning bolts. The minute you mess up – zap! – He will just burn you up like a little cinder.

He will not!

God is a good God, full of blessings, mercy, abundance, strength, health, victory, vitality, joy, peace, and security. He is a good God, and He cares for you! Until you get that in your spirit, you will constantly struggle with, "Is this God or is this the devil?"

We are going to draw the line; and everything that we can find that the devil has disrupted, we will make him put back on God's side of the line. We are not only going to make him stop, but we are going to make him get back across the line. We are none of the devil's business.

> **"We know that whosoever is born of God sinneth not; but he that is begotten of God keepeth himself, and that wicked one toucheth him not."**
>
> **1 John 5:18**

Notice it does not say someone else keepeth; it says keepeth himself. You present your body as a living sacrifice unto God, holy and acceptable, which is your reasonable service. Read that last part carefully: **"...but he that is begotten of God keepeth himself, and that wicked one toucheth him not."**

> **"Casting all your care upon him; for he careth for you. Be sober..."**
>
> **1 Peter 5:7-8**

Notice it does not say, "Be flaky." We are not talking about cereal Christians: fruits, flakes, and nuts. We are talking about being sober, not about getting out there in "lala" land.

> **"Be sober, be vigilant; because your adversary the devil..."**
>
> **1 Peter 5:8**

Notice it is not your wife, your mother-in-law, the banker, your boss, the pastor, the president, the economy, the homosexuals, or the pornographers.

You have one adversary – his name is the devil.

Know Your Authority

One of the major reasons Christians do not get victory over the devil is because they go off with some half-baked idea that they can just command the devil any way that they want.

The devil does not have to obey you when you lie.

People address the devil and say, "I rebuke you, Satan. I command you to go back to hell where you came from."

The devil is free to roam the world (2 Corinthians 4:4 refers to Satan as the god of this world). The only way you have authority over Satan is if you strive lawfully. You are no match for the devil, but **"...greater is he that is in you, than he that is in the world" (1**

John 4:4). You can make the devil get back on his side of the line and put back whatever he has stolen.

> **"...your adversary the devil, as a roaring lion..."**
>
> **1 Peter 5:8**

Notice it does not say he is a lion; it says he was AS a roaring lion. The devil only pretends to have the power of a lion. In fact, when his lie is exposed, he is a powder-puff lion.

> **"...walketh about..."**
>
> **1 Peter 5:8**

Zechariah 4:10 says, **"...the eyes of the Lord...run to and fro through the whole earth."** I like to serve the One who is running, not the one who is walking. Satan is walking and seeking. It does not say he found anyone; he cannot find you. If you stay out of the devil's territory, the evil one cannot touch you.

I am about to unfold something here that will stun you. Much of the reason that sickness hangs around your house is because you sit and feed your spirit out of that box in your living room that has horns and a tail that plugs into the wall – your television. You watch somebody else do what you would never do. The Word says not to even mention those things which they do in secret, not to even let them be named among you, much less be entertained by them.

> **"For it is a shame even to speak of those things which are done of them in secret."**
>
> **Ephesians 5:12**

We are not to take pleasure in the sin of others.
"My kids are sick."
I guess so!
"We don't seem to have much power."
I guess not.

"I'm timid and afraid."

You should be – you are what you feed yourself!

Dr. Lester Sumrall told me of a lady who came up in one of his services, needing deliverance from demon power. She was a junior church teacher in that local church; she taught the teenage class. Dr. Sumrall laid his hands on her and said, "Come out!"

A man's voice boiled up out of the inside of her. "I don't have to leave. She wants me here. I have a right to be here."

Sometimes when a demon is in operation, a man's voice will speak out of a woman or a woman's voice will speak out of a man. That is what happened to this woman.

Dr. Sumrall looked at her and said, "Did you hear that?"

She replied, "Yeah. I don't know who that voice was. I just can't sleep at night. I just came up here to get delivered."

So he laid his hands on her again and said, "Come out of her."

Up out of the inside of her, the voice spoke again. "I don't have to. She came into my territory. She gave me the right."

Dr. Sumrall asked her, "Is that right"

"Oh, no," she replied.

The man's voice came out of her saying, "Yes, you did. You came into the theater and watched that movie. You gave me the right."

She started to weep and cry. She had gone to an R-rated movie and tried to justify it by saying she just wanted to know what her teenagers were watching, what they were up against.

We always rationalize sin.

That voice said, "I have a right to stay here. She came on my territory."

I have news for you, beloved. It is time for us to stay on our side of the line. There is a line drawn. God said, **"...what fellowship hath righteousness with unrighteousness? and what communion hath light with darkness? (2 Corinthians 6:14).**

We must get on our side of the line so we can make the devil get back on his side of the line and put back what he has stolen.

Your Adversary the Devil

Let us take a look at our adversary.

> **"Moreover the word of the Lord came unto me, saying, Son of man, take up a lamentation upon the king of Tyrus, and say unto him, thus saith the Lord God; Thou sealest up the sum, full of wisdom, and perfect in beauty.**
>
> **"Thou hast been in Eden the garden of God; every precious stone was thy covering, the sardius, topaz, and the diamond, the Beryl, the onyx, and the jasper, the sapphire, the emerald, and the carbuncle, and gold: the workmanship of thy tabrets and of thy pipes was prepared in thee in the day that thou wast created."**
>
> **Ezekiel 28:11-13**

The devil in his original created form was a living, breathing instrument of praise to God. I suppose the closest thing that I have ever seen would be Phil Driscoll when he is under the anointing of God. His entire body is an instrument. It just seems that his whole being is an instrument and that God is playing upon him.

The Bible said that when Lucifer breathed, music would play through pipes that were created in his being. He was a living, moving, breathing instrument that brought praises unto the Lord.

Satan is now in a fallen state, but he is still making music. And his spirit is communicated through that music.

The devil is sowing his lies through music.

"Well, that's just a nice, sweet love song."

Well, who is singing it? What spirit are they of? What is being communicated to you?

There are even times when I have to turn off gospel music because it is the wrong spirit. It does not have anything to do with the beat; it does not have anything to do with the tempo – it simply is the wrong spirit.

Music is one of the most powerful forces known to man. You can drive people insane with music. You can drive people into a frenzy when Satan is in control. But when God gets in control, we can draw the line, lift our voices, and tell the devil to put it back.

We are not talking about some abstract design, some philosophic idea – we are talking about a created being. His name is Lucifer, the devil; and he is one of the only three archangels created in the heavens of God.

The Bible goes on and describes more about him in Ezekiel 28:14-16:

> **"Thou art the anointed cherub that covereth; and I have set thee so: thou wast upon the holy mountain of God; thou hast walked up and down in the midst of the stones of fire. Thou wast perfect in thy ways from the day that thou wast created, till iniquity was found in thee. By the multitude of thy merchandise..."**

Do you know what corrupted the devil? Merchandise. Lust for more. Greed. "I want. I will. I have a right."

Much of the church is getting corrupted by the multitude of their merchandise. Many denominations, as well as independent ministries, have stock on Wall Street or other investments for financial profit, but most do not have enough money free to preach the gospel to the heathen. It is all tied up. They are corrupted by the multitude of their merchandise.

People say, "Pastor, I can't be there on Wednesday night. I have to work" – and they are self-employed!

Merchandise – more and more.

That is the spirit of the world; it is not the spirit of God. We need to draw the line and tell the devil to put it back and get back on his side of the line.

Put it back how?

Put it back the way God wants it.

Some of you need to kick the devil onto the other side of the line and tell him to put it back. Some of you need to kick the devil out of your teenager's room and tell him to put it back.

Some of you need to kick the doubt, the cloudiness, the unbelief out of your mind and tell the devil to put it back the way God made it.

Some of you need to kick him out of your body with his manifestations and his residue. Tell him to put it back. He has stolen some of your dignity. You need to make him put it back. He has stolen some of your joy. You need to make him put it back.

> **"By the multitude of thy merchandise they have filled the midst of thee with violence, and thou hast sinned: therefore I will cast thee as profane out of the mountain of God: and I will destroy thee, O covering cherub, from the midst of the stones of fire."**
>
> **Ezekiel 28:16**

> **"Finally, my brethren, be strong in the Lord, and in the power of his might. Put on the whole armour of God..."**
>
> **Ephesians 6:10-11**

The scripture says the whole armour, not just the helmet of salvation. Most of the Body of Christ goes into battle completely naked, except for a helmet on top of their head. Where is the shield of faith? The sword of the Spirit? The breastplate of righteousness? Why are your loins not girded about with truth? Where is the pre-par-ation of the gospel of peace?

You need more than a helmet.

> **"Put on the whole armour of God, that ye may be able to stand against the wiles of the devil. For we wrestle not against flesh and blood, but against principalities, against powers, against the rulers of the**

darkness of this world, against spiritual wickedness in high places.

"Wherefore take unto you the whole armour of God, that ye may be able to withstand in the evil day, and having done all, to stand.

"Stand therefore, having your loins girt about with truth, and having on the breastplate of righteousness; And your feet shod with the preparation of the gospel of peace; Above all, taking the shield of faith, wherewith ye shall be able..." Not may be able. "...ye shall be able to quench all the fiery darts of the wicked.

"And take the helmet of salvation, and the sword of the Spirit, which is the word of God: Praying always with all prayer and supplication in the Spirit, and watching thereunto with all perseverance and supplication for all saints."

Ephesians 6:11-18

Our warfare is not carnal.

"(For the weapons of our warfare are not carnal, but mighty through God to the pulling down of strong holds;) Casting down imaginations, and every high thing that exalteth itself against the knowledge of God..."

2 Corinthians 10:4-5

The Spirit of God is speaking to my heart that you need to make the devil put it back. Let him that stole steal no more. It is time something rose up on the inside of you and commanded, "Devil, put it back! Put my joy back. Put my hope back. Put my victory back. Put my shout back. Put the glory back. Do not just leave, Devil – put it back!"

How Did We Get Here?

Sometimes it is helpful to understand how we got in such a mess. If we can understand that, then we can avoid the same pitfalls in the future.

In Mark 5:1-2 we read,

> **"And they came over unto the other side of the sea, into the country of the Gadarenes. And when he [Jesus] was come out of the ship, immediately there met him out of the tombs a man with an unclean spirit."**

I wonder how that spirit entered. How did he get in this condition? I wonder where it was he stepped over the line. I wonder where the protective covering of God was lifted. I wonder where he backed across the line that God laid down.

> **"Wherefore come out from among them, and be ye separate, saith the Lord..."**
>
> **2 Corinthians 6:17**

We are to separate ourselves unto the Lord and be holy.

Somewhere, somehow, we all have let the devil in – maybe in a moment of weakness, maybe in a moment of trial, maybe in a moment of temptation, maybe through ignorance. I do not know when it was; I do not know where it was; I do not know how it was – but it is time to get him back across the line.

The evil one cannot touch you.

> **"...a man with an unclean spirit, Who had his dwelling among the tombs; and no man could bind him, no, not with chains."**
>
> **Mark 5:2-3**

Like so many of us, there was no natural help for this man. No psychologist or sociologist on the face of the earth could massage his brain with their intellect.

Nothing could free that man.

There is only one thing that can get you or that man across the line, and His name is Jesus.

The man could not even be bound with chains.

> **"Because that he had been often bound with fetters and chains, and the chains had been plucked asunder by him, and the fetters broken in pieces: neither could any man tame him. And always, night and day, he was in the mountains, and in the tombs, crying, and cutting himself with stones."**
>
> **Mark 5:4-5**

Man is bent on self-destruction. The things we want the most destroy us the quickest. Why does your natural man crave coconut cream pie more than an apple? Because an apple is better for you.

Sometimes Christians let that spirit of the world filter in, and they get all tangled up in the merchandise. Somehow they slip back across the line, and the evil one begins to touch them. It is nasty on the other side of the line.

This man with an unclean spirit cut himself with stones and lived in the graveyard.

Today, there are a whole lot of people milling around in the spiritual graveyards, in past blessings, past revelation, a past touch of God, a past movement of the Spirit of God.

Let me ask you point blank: "When is the last time the Holy Ghost moved on you? Where is your life? Your light? Could it be you have drifted back across the line?

Look what happened to this fellow.

> **"And always, night and day, he was in the mountains, and in the tombs, crying, and cutting**

himself with stones. But when he saw Jesus afar off, he ran and worshipped him, And cried with a loud voice, and said, What have I to do with thee, Jesus, thou Son of the most high God? I adjure thee by God, that thou torment me not."

Mark 5:5-7

Do you see it? Even the demons know God!

You can get known in the realm of the spirit.

"...What have I to do with thee, Jesus..." they cried out.

"Well, yes, that is true in this passage. But Jesus was the Son of God. What happened to Him could never happen to me."

Why not? Are you a cauliflower? He has given you the power to become sons of God.

He called His disciples together and gave them power over all devils and to cure diseases.

I am so glad Jesus did not say, "You have power over some of the devils." Can you imagine how difficult it would be for us to decide which ones we could make leave and which ones would have to stay?

Thankfully, He said, I give you **"...power and authority over all devils, and to cure diseases"** (Luke 9:1).

The demons pleaded, **"I adjure thee by God, that thou torment me not"** (Mark 5:7).

Jesus did not have anything pleasant in mind for the devil. He was not going to give him lodging, or pet him, or make him comfortable.

"For he [Jesus] said unto him, Come out of the man, thou unclean spirit."

Mark 5:8

When is the last time you talked like that to the enemy?

"And he asked him, What is thy name? And he answered, saying, My name is Legion: for we are many.

Mark 5:9

You have to understand the only reason he did not lie to Jesus was because Jesus was operating in the gift of discernment.

If you ask the devil how many he is, he'll say, "15,000," when there is only one little puny devil. He is the king of all liars, the father of all lies. He is not going to tell you the truth.

The only thing you need to tell the devil is to get out and put it back.

Problems or Demons?

Some time back when I was in Washington, D.C., God spoke to me and said, "You need to begin to preach more about demon power."

"Why is that?" I asked the Lord.

"Because the church is full of it," He told me.

We call it "our problem."

The only problem we have is the devil.

"Well, my wife and I have a problem."

No, you do not have a problem. It is the devil, and it is time to make him get back on his side of the line and put it back.

When Christians are getting divorced at the same rate as those in the world, that is called demon power. I believe the major reason people get divorced is because they are full of selfishness. They make little babies grow up without both parents. You know I am telling the truth. We need to quit making the atmosphere of our homes conducive for the manifestations of hell.

If you fill your home with the praises of God, the devil will be nervous about hanging around. Fill your home with the joy of the Lord and victory.

Get up every morning and say, "Devil, we're awake." Notify every devil of hell that you know the greater One is in you and the devil had better not even dare to try and cross that line with poverty, sickness, disease, hurt, tragedy, or accidents.

Some of you need to get your health put back.

Stop looking for the philosophic, abstract answers. The devil is not abstract; he is real! He has been walking around Christian houses for years.

"How do you know?"

I see his manifestations everywhere! It is time to make him get out of your home.

"Well, I don't know how. Why don't you tell me how."

I am glad you asked.

Kicking the Devil Out

"Therefore if any man be in Christ, he is a new creature: old things are passed away; behold, all things are become new."

2 Corinthians 5:17

Are you in Christ? That means the devil is on the other side of the line. All things on your side of the line are of God.

"And all things are of God, who hath reconciled us to himself by Jesus Christ, and hath given to us the ministry of reconciliation."

2 Corinthians 5:18

The book of Acts is where the God in Christ becomes the Christ in you.

"...greater is he that is in you, than he that is in the world."

1 John 4:4

By the power of the Holy Ghost, you have the awesome authority, in the name of Jesus, to tell the devil what to do. Dwight Thompson's wife gets up every morning and says, "Devil, I'm going to give you permission today to do one thing – look at the bottom of my feet." She is really saying, "Get on your side of the line, and put it back."

149

"...and hath committed unto us the word of reconciliation. Now then we are ambassadors for Christ, as
though God did beseech you by us: we pray you in
Christ's stead, be ye reconciled to God."

2 Corinthians 5:19-20

You now speak in Christ's place.

"To whom ye forgive any thing, I forgive also: for
if I forgave any thing, to whom I forgave it, for your
sakes forgave I it in the person of Christ."

2 Corinthians 2:10

Here is the important part.

Paul said, "When I forgive, it is not me forgiving; it is Christ in
me forgiving."

"Now thanks be unto God, which always causeth
us to triumph in Christ, and maketh manifest the savour of his knowledge by us in every place. For we are
unto God a sweet savour of Christ..."

"For we are not as many, which corrupt the word
of God: but as of sincerity, but as of God, in the sight
of God speak we in Christ."

2 Corinthians 2:14,15,17

Are you allowing these truths to flow into your spirit? You are
just about ready to make the devil get back on the side of his line
and put it back.

When you command him, it is not you commanding at all.
Greater is He that lives on the inside of you than he that is in the
world!

Alone, you are no match for the devil.

But you are not alone!

If you would say to me, "The devil has been trying to put things on me; the devil has made a mess of my life," then I would say to you, "Square your shoulders; take your stand and say, 'Satan, get back on your side of the line. I command you, in Jesus' name, to get out and put back everything you have taken!'"

Endnotes

[1] Walter B. Knight, *Knight's Master Book of New Illustrations* (Grand Rapids: Eerdman's Printing Company, 1956), p. 561.

[2] Lester Sumrall, *Exorcism: The Reality of Evil...and Your Power Over It!* (Arkansas: New Leaf Press, 1991), pp. 38,39.

[3] U.S. Department of Health and Human Services (2005). Indicators of Welfare Dependence. Annual Report to Congress 2005. Table Birth 1, Washington, D.C.

[4] *Webster's Third New International Dictionary,* s.v. "omni."

[5] *Ibid.,* s.v. "potent."

Your Freedom Tool Kit

Here Are the Tools, the Spiritual Hammer and Nails, You Need to Biblically Repair the Freedom Plank in Your Life.

I. **Cain (Sin Is at the Door); Sin Keeps You in Bondage**

Genesis 4:3 And in process of time it came to pass, that Cain brought of the fruit of the ground an offering unto the Lord.

v. 4 And Abel, he also brought of the firstlings of his flock and of the fat thereof. And the Lord had respect unto Abel and to his offering.

v. 5 But unto Cain and to his offering he had not respect. And Cain was very wroth, and his countenance fell.

v. 6 And the Lord said unto Cain, Why art thou wroth? and why is thy countenance fallen?

v. 7 If thou doest well, shalt thou not be accepted? and if thou doest not well, sin lieth at the door. And unto thee shall be his desire, and thou shalt rule over him.

II. **Demonic Activity as a Result of Sin**

1 Samuel 28:7 Then said Saul unto his servants, Seek me a woman that hath a familiar spirit, that I may go to her, and inquire of her. And his servants said to him, Behold, there is a woman that hath a familiar spirit at Endor.

III. Financial Bondage as a Result of Sin

Matthew 19:16 And , behold, one came and said unto him, Good Master, what good thing shall I do, that I may have eternal life?

v. 17 And he said unto him, Why callest thou me good? there is none good but one, that is, God: but if thou wilt enter into life, keep the commandments.

v. 18 He saith unto him, Which? Jesus said, Thou shalt do no murder, Thou shalt not commit adultery, Thou shalt not steal, Thou shalt not bear false witness,

v. 19 Honour thy father and thy mother: and, Thou shalt love thy neighbour as thyself.

v. 20 The young man saith unto him, All these things have I kept from my youth up: what lack I yet?

v. 21 Jesus said unto him, If thou wilt be perfect, go and sell that thou hast, and give to the poor, and thou shalt have treasure in heaven: and come and follow me.

v. 22 But when the young man heard that saying, he went away sorrowful: for he had great possessions.

v. 23 Then said Jesus unto his disciples, Verily I say unto you, That a rich man shall hardly enter into the kingdom of heaven.

v. 24 And again I say unto you, It is easier for a camel to go through the eye of a needle, than for a rich man to enter into the kingdom of God.

IV. Deliverance Comes From God

Psalm 27:1 The Lord is my light and my salvation; whom shall I fear? the Lord is the strength of my life; of whom shall I be afraid?

v. 2 When the wicked, even mine enemies and my foes, came upon me to eat up my flesh, they stumbled and fell.

v. 3 Though an host should encamp against me, my heart shall not fear: though war should rise against me, in this will I be confident.

v. 5 For in the time of trouble he shall hide me in his pavilion: in the secret of his tabernacle shall he hide me; he shall set me up upon a rock.

Psalm 32:7 Thou art my hiding place; thou shalt preserve me from trouble; thou shalt compass me about with songs of deliverance. Selah.

Psalm 119:45 And I will walk at liberty: for I seek thy precepts.

Joel 2:32 And it shall come to pass, that whosoever shall call on the name of the Lord shall be delivered: for in mount Zion and in Jerusalem shall be deliverance, as the Lord hath said, and in the remnant whom the Lord shall call.

Obadiah 1:17 But upon mount Zion shall be deliverance, and there shall be holiness; and the house of Jacob shall possess their possessions.

Isaiah 61:1 The Spirit of the Lord God is upon me; because the Lord hath anointed me to preach good tidings unto the meek; he hath sent me to bind up the brokenhearted, to proclaim liberty to the captives, and the opening of the prison to them that are bound.

1 Samuel 16:23 And it came to pass, when the evil spirit from God was upon Saul, that David took an harp, and played with his hand: so Saul was refreshed, and was well, and the evil spirit departed from him.

Micah 4:1 But in the last days it shall come to pass, that the mountain of the house of the Lord shall be established in the top of the mountains, and it shall be exalted above the hills; and people shall flow unto it.

v. 2 And many nations shall come, and say, Come, and let us go up to the mountain of the Lord, and to the house of the God of Jacob; and he will teach us of his ways, and we will walk in his paths: for the law shall go forth of Zion, and the word of the Lord from Jerusalem.

Matthew 6:31 Therefore take no thought, saying, What shall we eat? or, What shall we drink? or, Wherewithal shall we be clothed?

v. 32 (For after all these things do the Gentiles seek:) for your heavenly Father knoweth that ye have need of all these things.

v. 33 But seek ye first the kingdom of God, and his righteousness; and all these things shall be added unto you.

v. 34 Take therefore no thought for the morrow: for the morrow shall take thought for the things of itself. Sufficient unto the day is the evil thereof.

Luke 4:18 The Spirit of the Lord is upon me, because he hath anointed me to preach the gospel to the poor; he hath sent me to heal the brokenhearted, to preach deliverance to the captives, and recovering of sight to the blind, to set at liberty them that are bruised,

v. 19 To preach the acceptable year of the Lord.

John 16:33 These things I have spoken unto you, that in me ye might have peace. In the world ye shall have tribulation: but be of good cheer; I have overcome the world.

John 8:32 And ye shall know the truth, and the truth shall make you free.

v. 33 They answered him, We be Abraham's seed, and were never in bondage to any man: how sayest thou, Ye shall be made free?

v. 34 Jesus answered them, Verily, verily, I say unto you, Whosoever committeth sin is the servant of sin.

v. 35 And the servant abideth not in the house for ever: but the Son abideth ever.

v. 36 If the Son therefore shall make you free, ye shall be free indeed.

Romans 6:6 Knowing this, that our old man is crucified with him, that the body of sin might be destroyed, that henceforth we should not serve sin.

v. 7 For he that is dead is freed from sin.

Romans 6:20 For when ye were the servants of sin, ye were free from righteousness.

v. 21 What fruit had ye then in those things whereof ye are now ashamed? for the end of those things is death.

v. 22 But now being made free from sin, and become servants to God, ye have your fruit unto holiness, and the end everlasting life.

Romans 8:1 There is therefore now no condemnation to them which are in Christ Jesus, who walk not after the flesh, but after the Spirit.

v. 2 For the law of the Spirit of life in Christ Jesus hath made me free from the law of sin and death.

Romans 8:21 Because the creature itself also shall be delivered from the bondage of corruption into the glorious liberty of the children of God.

Hebrews 11:35 Women received their dead raised to life again: and others were tortured, not accepting deliverance; that they might obtain a better resurrection.

Galatians 3:28 There is neither Jew nor Greek, there is neither bond nor free, there is neither male nor female: for ye are all one in Christ Jesus.

Galatians 5:1 Stand fast therefore in the liberty wherewith Christ hath made us free, and be not entangled again with the yoke of bondage.

Galatians 5:13 For, brethren, ye have been called unto liberty; only use not liberty for an occasion to the flesh, but by love serve one another.

James 1:25 But whoso looketh into the perfect law of liberty, and continueth therein, he being not a forgetful hearer, but a doer of the work, this man shall be blessed in his deed.

2 Corinthians 3:17 Now the Lord is that Spirit: and where the Spirit of the Lord is, there is liberty.

PLANK FOUR

Restoring Power to the
Body of Christ

PLANK FOUR

Restoring Power to the Body of Christ

There for the Taking

I left the prayer meeting and crept out into the lane away from town. As I walked, I said, "Oh, my God, if there is a man who needs the power of the Holy Ghost to rest upon him, it is I; but I do not know how to receive Him. I am too tired, too worn, too nervously down to agonize."

A voice said to me, "As you took forgiveness from the hand of the dying Christ, take the Holy Ghost from the hand of the living Christ."

I turned to Christ and said, "Lord, I breathe in this whiff of warm night air, so I breathe into every part of me thy blessed Spirit." I felt no hand laid upon my head, there was no lambent flame, there was no rushing sound from heaven; but by faith, without emotion, without excitement, I took, and took for the first time, and I have kept on taking ever since.

– F.B. Meyer,
in The Overcomer[1]

He who neglects to obey the command to be filled with the Spirit, is as guilty of breaking the command of God, as he who steals, or curses, or commits adultery. His guilt is as great as the authority of God is great, who commands us to be filled. His guilt is equivalent to all the good he might do if he were filled with the Spirit.

– Charles G. Finney
in Elim Evangel[2]

Puttering and Sputtering…in Power?

We shout "Greater is He that is in me than he that is in the world," yet we cannot pray away a simple headache. We dab a little oil on our foreheads, say a quick prayer, then sneak away and take two aspirin when no one is looking.

We claim, "My God owns the cattle on a thousand hills;" yet, we wallow in debt and bankruptcy, too poor to finance the gospel and bring its life-saving message to the billions of lost souls floundering in our world. The church sputters along, holding meetings and seminars about the miracle-working power of God, only to have members of the congregation run out between services for a quick cigarette or a beer.

The devil has stolen our power.

The church putters in end-time evangelism – claiming lack of money, lack of manpower, lack of organization between denominations. The real truth is, we are powerless because we wallow in sin, secretly failing to renounce the lies, the adultery, the child abuse, and the other hidden sins that the devil uses to rob us of our power.

I am so tired of philosophical mish-mash, of Pentecostal churches talking in tongues only in the Sunday night service where they think it is "safe" and they will not offend anyone.

I am so tired of preachers refusing to speak against divorce for fear that any "remarrieds" in the congregation might refuse to tithe.

Where are God's men of power, men who preach not by congregational consensus, but by the pure, unaltered Word of God?

Where are the signs?
The wonders?
The miracles?
The lost souls being led to salvation?

The power of the church has been stolen by the devil's lies. Today, I want to declare it is time to put Holy Ghost POWER back into our theology!

The reason Jacob wrestled all night with the angel of the Lord is that there was too much Jacob and not enough God. Today, there is too much Jacob and not enough God in the church. We must decrease so He can increase!

> **"...When the day of Pentecost was fully come, they were all with one accord in one place. And suddenly there came a sound from heaven as of a rushing mighty wind, and it filled all the house where they were sitting. And there appeared unto them cloven tongues like as of fire, and it sat upon each of them. And they were all filled with the Holy Ghost, and began to speak with other tongues, as the Spirit gave them utterance."**
>
> **Acts 2:1-4**

We have been flopping around like guppies in a little pool of spiritual blessing when God wants us to be as spiritual sharks in a mighty, roaring ocean.

The Methodist campground used to be the most fire-filled place around.

John Wesley, founder of the Methodist movement, once said, "I do not fear that Methodism and the people called Methodists will ever cease to exist; but I do fear that in existing they will become a dead sect, having a form of godliness, but denying the power thereof. If Methodism is ever overthrown, it will be at the hands of our scholars and theologians who neither believe her doctrines nor practice her policy. It is from these men that it must cleanse itself or fall by its own weight."

That powerful statement can be true of any move of God! It is time for Pentecostals to start acting like Pentecostals – walking in the power of Pentecost! It is time we once again become tongue-talking, on-fire Christians who allow the gifts of the Spirit back into our theology and into our lives.

Let's Get Drunk!

I am tired of a church that just takes a little sip of the Holy Ghost. It is time to drink in the whole experience, the entire package God has to offer!

It is time to get skunk drunk on the Holy Ghost to the point where everyone looks good and Jesus is in control.

People who are drunk in the natural world see things no one else sees, and they hear voices no one else hears.

To the spiritually dead, God does not speak.

To the spiritually dead, God does not live.

But to the spiritually alive, we see things no one else sees.

We see victory in the middle of defeat!

We see healing in the presence of disease and distress!

Let's get drunk, filled with the Holy Ghost, so we can hear Him start talking.

Have you ever noticed that when someone is drunk, they never run from a fight? I believe when we are a church skunk drunk on the Holy Ghost, we will not run from the devil but instead will spit in his eye and say, "take that, Devil; you are defeated!"

I want to see Christians who have spiritually crooked noses, who have a few scars over their eyebrows, who have knuckles broken in several places – all because they dove headfirst into confrontation with the devil, and bloodied him good in the process.

I am tired of a Holy Ghost who must be socially acceptable so we do not offend the "first-timers" coming to our churches. The church is sputtering and puttering in pretend power, ministering a mediocre, mundane, weak-kneed, spineless gospel.

When people get drunk, they drop their inhibitions. They even take off their clothes.

I believe it is time for the church to strip off our old clothes, our garments soiled and stained with sin. Let us throw off our religious badges and denominational uniforms and go bare before God! Let us cast aside the garments of this world and put on the vesture of the garments of holiness and purity before God. The apostles became drunk in the Holy Ghost. They were so full of God that Peter had to assure the men of Jerusalem that they were not physically drunk.

> **"For these are not drunken, as ye suppose, seeing it is but the third hour of the day.**
>
> **"But this is that which was spoken by the prophet Joel;**
>
> **"And I will show wonders in heaven above, and signs in the earth beneath; blood, and fire, and vapour of smoke."**
>
> **Acts 2:15,16,19**

Did Peter say, "Hey, fellows, let's tone this thing down. Our fire and smoke might scare away a few people"? Of course not.

Instead, the apostles manifested God's power and brought 8,000 to the Lord at the time of Pentecost.

When a person is drunk, they often want to cry. Many of you have heard a crying drunk slobber and stammer and tell you how much he loves you before he falls over.

Jeremiah was called the weeping prophet because he looked out over the kingdom of Israel and cried and wept before the Lord.

Let's take the mask off.

When was the last time you looked out upon a world of billions of lost souls and cried before the Lord for His mercy, His compassion, His empowerment to reach the suffering masses destined for eternal flames?

Get drunk in the Holy Ghost, and you will do that. You will experience the compassion of Jesus. Your heart will melt in the hand of a God who has the nail prints to prove He died for you, and for the whole world. Lord, let the tears flow from our eyes. Let us weep again.

Give us prophets who cry out for America. Give us a weeping clergy willing to spill tears over the sins of their people. Give us somebody to weep over the murders of millions of innocent babies. Give us prayer warriors who will cry for the prostitutes, the cocaine addicts, the gang members.

Lord, give us tears.

Let us get drunk on the Holy Ghost.

Do you know why the bars stay open until 3:00 in the morning?

Because no one cares when they go home!

I think it is time we turned the church into a place where no one cares when they go home, a place where the power of God flows so strongly in our services that we forget not just the minute, but the hour!

When you get drunk in the Holy Ghost, your spiritual pride will die. You will dance in the aisles; you will run through the streets; you will jump over every obstacle. David was a king; yet, he danced before the Lord with all of his energy and passion.

It is time we stopped being nice.

Settled.

Predictable.

It is time to do flip-flops in the church aisles, to stop being ashamed, to let the Lord crucify your pride so you have no embarrassment.

We serve Jesus, the lion of the tribe of Judah.

We have soul satisfaction.

Our sins are washed away, and we are on our way to heaven.

That deserves more shouting than a touchdown, more jumping up and down than when receiving a monetary inheritance, and more dancing than at a high school prom.

When we get drunk in the Holy Ghost, then every homosexual will hear the message that God has the power to set them free; every murderer will know God loves them; every prostitute will renounce the flesh for the Spirit.

Church, let's get drunk and let the Lord transform us through the power of the Holy Ghost!

The Wind Is Blowing

It is time to experience demonstrations in power, preaching on the manifestation of tongues and interpretation of tongues, on prophecy, on the word of wisdom, on the word of knowledge, on discerning of spirits, on wonder-working faith, on the gift of the working of miracles, and on the gifts of healings.

If the church wants to see revival, it will start when we get the Holy Ghost and His gifts back into our theology and our lives.

> **"For as many as are led by the Spirit of God, they are the sons of God."**
>
> **Romans 8:14**

You are a son of God.

> **"And suddenly there came a sound from heaven as of a rushing mighty wind, and it filled all the house where they were sitting."**
>
> **Acts 2:2**

A mighty wind roared upon God's sons at Pentecost.

> **"The wind bloweth where it listeth, and thou hearest the sound thereof, but canst not tell whence it cometh, and whither it goeth: so is every one that is born of the Spirit."**
>
> **John 3:8**

The wind blows where it wants to. You hear the sound of it, you see the effects, but you cannot tell where it comes from or where it is going.

That is the way it is when you receive the baptism in the Holy Ghost. When you relax into the flow of the Holy Spirit, God places you where He wants you. You may find yourself in the most incredible place doing something you never dreamed possible. Wherever you go or whatever you do, it will be thrilling beyond your wildest dreams.

When the wind of the Holy Ghost begins to blow, something is about to happen; something is about to change. The leaves begin to turn over; the daffodils pull back in and recoil. They know something is about to happen. When the winds begin to blow, the finest of vines will begin to wrap itself and entwine itself around the base of a mighty oak and hold on.

Something is about to happen.

When John the Baptist was baptizing in the River Jordan after coming out of the wilderness where he ate locusts and wild honey, the Bible tells us,

"John did baptize in the wilderness, and preach the baptism of repentance for the remission of sins."

Mark 1:4

But, John knew another level of spiritual experience was possible.

"...There cometh one mightier than I after me, the latchet of whose shoes I am not worthy to stoop down and unloose. I indeed have baptized you with water: but he shall baptize you with the Holy Ghost."

Mark 1:7-8

All church members and sinners alike should know about the baptism in the Holy Ghost. Everyone should know that God said, "I'm going to baptize you in the Holy Ghost and fire."

The Holy Ghost baptism is an experience subsequent to your salvation that will change you. The devil will not be able to stand you when you become baptized in the Holy Ghost.

You may say, "Now, wait a minute. I'm already a Christian. I'm born again; I've accepted the blood of Jesus Christ as the full payment for my sins, so I must have the Holy Ghost."

Please understand, I am not writing about HAVING the Holy Ghost; I am writing about the Holy Ghost having you, taking charge of your life so that you are absolutely possessed by the Spirit of the living God. In the last days, the Bible tells us that the works of the flesh will be manifest.

> **"Now the works of the flesh are manifest, which are these; Adultery, fornication, uncleanness, lasciviousness, idolatry, witchcraft, hatred, variance, emulations, wrath, strife, seditions, heresies, envyings, murders, drunkenness, revellings, and such like..."**
>
> **Galatians 5:19-21**

Clearly, these works are manifest in the day and age in which we live.

You Decide What You Want

You can sit in your little world, governed by the dictates of your own mind, and play church and soothe your conscience while the world is going to hell.

Or you can determine this day, "I am going to get everything God promised me. I am going to become endued with power from on high.

God said that in the last days

> **"...I will pour out my spirit upon all flesh; and your sons and your daughters shall prophesy, your old men shall dream dreams, your young men shall see visions: And also upon the servants and upon the handmaids in those days will I pour out my spirit."**
>
> **Joel 2:28-29**

In John 14, Jesus had told His disciples, "I'm going to leave here, but I will not leave you alone. There's One coming after Me I will send to comfort you, to help you. I will send you the blessed Third Person of the Trinity. He shall dwell inside you, and the same Spirit that raised Me up from the dead will quicken your mortal bodies and make you alive and full of power."

In Acts 1:8, it says **"But ye shall receive power"** – power to resist temptation, power to resist sin, power to be all God intends for your life.

You can receive the power to lift your hands boldly and declare, "The kingdom of God is at hand," the power to be a testimony to your family members, the power to see cancer dry up and wither in your body, the power to walk circumspectly in the earth!

In Acts 2, it says on the day of Pentecost, there was a mighty sound from heaven. That wind did not come from the headquarters of a denominational general assembly. It did not come out of a man, out of a building, or out of an organization.

The baptism in the Holy Ghost and fire and power comes straight from heaven!

Many of you are going to break out of the chains of religion. God is going to loose your tongue to speak in other tongues. You are going to be begging God for somebody with whom to share your faith in Jesus Christ.

You say, "but that's not me; that's not the way I am."

I am telling you, God will change you so much you will look in the mirror and not even recognize yourself. He will set you on fire with the things of God; He will give you a love for the Word of God that is insatiable; He will give you a hunger and desire for the church of Jesus Christ and fellowship with the saints that cannot be quenched.

It is time that the church started acting like the New Testament was true. We need to become fanatical – to start smiling, jumping, and shouting, lifting our hands to heaven, and talking in tongues to our Creator. It is time we pull out all the spiritual stops and get completely filled with the joy, the love, the compassion, and the miracle-working power of God!

The Bible says, "You will be baptized in the Holy Ghost." When you are baptized in the Holy Ghost, something – or rather someone – gets you. You cannot see you anymore. It is God above you, God beneath you, God in the middle of you. The church needs a dynamic outpouring of the Spirit of God until the world does not see us anymore.

Immersed In Him

To baptize means "to submerge fully."

God wants to immerse you, to overshadow your life with His power so that you can transcend the natural realm. He wants to fill you and flood you and baptize you into Himself, to give you power over all devils, all sickness, and all sin.

The wind of the Holy Ghost will start to flow into you at the top of your head and shoot out the bottom of your feet. Like a mighty whirlwind, He will go through you and change you into another human being, enabling you to speak in other tongues, to prophesy, to operate in the gifts of healing and revelation.

On the day of Pentecost, there came a sound from heaven as of a rushing, mighty wind. That same wind is available to you today – the wind of the Holy Ghost.

You may say, "But I don't understand it."

You do not have to understand it; just give in.

What About Tongues?

"...there came a sound from heaven as of a rushing mighty wind, and it filled all the house where they were sitting. And there appeared unto them cloven tongues like as of fire, and it sat upon each of them. And they were all filled with the Holy Ghost, and began to speak with other tongues, as the Spirit gave them utterance."

Acts 2:2-4

Many Christians do not understand the speaking in other tongues.

Let me explain.

171

Man is a spirit who lives in a body and possesses a soul. The spirit of man came directly from God. The soul and body were created, but the spirit came directly from God. Then man transgressed the law of God in Genesis 3, and sin entered into the picture. Man had originally been directed and dictated by his spirit that came directly from God. When he chose to eat of the fruit of the tree of the knowledge of good and evil, the spirit went into the background, and man became dominated by his soul, which is his mind, will, and emotions.

His mind told his body what to do, and his spirit was silent.

When you get baptized in the Holy Ghost and you start praying in tongues, people might say, "You've lost your mind," to which you reply, "That's right; my mind is no longer in control; my body is submitting to my spirit. I am speaking words that are not in contact with my mind. I am a spirit being recreated in the image of God, baptized with the Holy Ghost and fire.

Many Christians have been dabbling in the Holy Ghost. Every now and then they speak in other tongues, but they do not have much power in their lives.

It is time for you to start overflowing! Let God grab you by the spiritual head and plunge you into the depths of His very own being.

Do you want to be at the bottom of the depths of God? Do you want to get lost in God? Do you want God to totally surround and supersede every other thing in your life? Do you want to get filled inside and surrounded by God?

He promised it to you. He said, "I will baptize you in the Holy Ghost and fire."

The word "baptize" means "to submerge fully."

Just Do It!

To my knowledge, I have never prayed for anyone to receive the baptism of the Holy Ghost who did not receive it. Do not let the issue of tongues stop you. I am talking about a baptism of fire and power.

Yes, the initial evidence is speaking with other tongues – a language you never spoke and do not understand.

The Bible says they **"...began to speak with other tongues, as the Spirit gave them utterance" (Acts 2:4)**. Another way of saying that same thing would be, "as the Spirit of God enabled them to express their original selves (or your spirit)."

The Spirit of God does the enabling; He does not do the speaking. Do not expect God to grab your tongue and wiggle it and push in and out on your diaphragm. God is not going to do that.

On the inside of you, you will sense something prompting you to say words and syllables. Just open up your mouth and let the words flow. I do not care if it is "la, la, la," or "da, da, da."

The devil hates it all.

John 7:38 states that rivers of living water will flow out of you.

The river is the Holy Ghost.

It is time to kick the rocks off the well of your life and let the river flow. When it happens, when the well of your life becomes a river, you are covered by that flow. Like a spring at the bottom of a lake, you continue to pour out the flow of God; you become the head waters of a mighty river that will bring life everywhere it flows.

First, it will quicken (give life to) your spirit, then your soul (mind, will, and emotions), then your body, and then your family, and then your world.

Endnotes

[1] Walter B. Knight, *Knight's Master Book of New Illustrations* (Grand Rapids: Eerdman's Printing Co., 1957), p. 287.

[2] *Ibid.*

Your Baptism of the Holy Spirit Tool Kit

Here Are the Tools, the Spiritual Hammer and Nails, You Need to Biblically Repair and Restore the Power Plank in Your Life.

The baptism of the Holy Spirit is available to all New Testament believers and is an essential element in winning the world to the Lord Jesus Christ.

I.   Subsequent to Salvation

The Holy Spirit Comes to Dwell Within Every Believer When They Receive Jesus Christ as Savior and Lord

Romans 8:16 The Spirit itself beareth witness with our spirit, that we are the children of God.

The Baptism of the Holy Spirit Is Something Different That Happens After Salvation

John 4:14 But whosoever drinketh of the water that I shall give him shall never thirst; but the water that I shall give him shall be in him a well of water springing up into everlasting life.

John 7:38 He that believeth on me, as the scripture hath said, out of his belly shall flow rivers of living water.

174

Acts 8:5 Then Philip went down to the city of Samaria, and preached Christ unto them.

v. 6 And the people with one accord gave heed unto those things which Philip spake, hearing and seeing the miracles which he did.

v 7 For unclean spirits, crying with loud voice, came out of many that were possessed with them: and many taken with palsies, and that were lame, were healed.

v 8 And there was great joy in that city.

v 9 But there was a certain man, called Simon, which beforetime in the same city used sorcery, and bewitched the people of Samaria, giving out that himself was some great one:

v. 10 To whom they all gave heed, from the least to the greatest, saying, This man is the great power of God.

v 11 And to him they had regard, because that of long time he had bewitched them with sorceries.

v 12 But when they believed Philip preaching the things concerning the kingdom of God, and the name of Jesus Christ, they were baptized, both men and women.

v. 13 Then Simon himself believed also: and when he was baptized, he continued with Philip, and wondered, beholding the miracles and signs which were done.

v 14 Now when the apostles which were at Jerusalem heard that Samaria had received the word of God, they sent unto them Peter and John:

v. 15 Who, when they were come down, prayed for them, that they might receive the Holy Ghost:

v. 16 (For as yet he was fallen upon none of them: only they were baptized in the name of the Lord Jesus.)

v. 17 Then laid they their hands on them, and they re-ceived the Holy Ghost.

II. For Every Believer

Are You a River or a Reservoir?

John 7:38 He that believeth on me, as the scripture hath said, out of his belly shall flow rivers of living water.

Don't Go Anywhere Until You Are Endued With Power

Luke 24:49 And, behold, I send the promise of my Father upon you: but tarry ye in the city of Jerusalem, until ye be endued with power from on high.

This Promise Is for Everyone

Acts 2:39 For the promise is unto you, and to your children, and to all that are afar off, even as many as the Lord our God shall call.

It Is One of the Purposes of Jesus' Ministry to You

Luke 3:16 John answered, saying unto them all, I indeed baptize you with water, but one mightier than I cometh, the latchet of whose shoes I am not worthy to unloose: he shall baptize you with the Holy Ghost and with fire.

III. Three Ingredients

The candidate – You

The element – The Holy Spirit

The baptizer – Jesus Christ

IV. Baptism of the Holy Spirit — Purpose

Power to Be a Witness

Acts 1:8 But ye shall receive power, after that the Holy Ghost is come upon you: and ye shall be witnesses unto me both in Jerusalem, and in all Judaea, and in Samaria, and unto the uttermost part of the earth.

Other Benefits

New Perspective on the Things of God

John 16:13 Howbeit when he, the Spirit of truth, is come, he will guide you into all truth: for he shall not speak of himself; but whatsoever he shall hear, that shall he speak: and he will show you things to come.

Access to All the Gifts of the Spirit

1 Corinthians 12:8 For to one is given by the Spirit the word of wisdom; to another the word of knowledge by the same Spirit;

v. 9 To another faith by the same Spirit; to another the gifts of healing by the same Spirit;

v. 10 To another the working of miracles; to another prophecy; to another discerning of spirits; to another divers kinds of tongues; to another the interpretation of tongues.

Speaking in Tongues ("Prayer Language")

1 Corinthians 14:4 He that speaketh in an unknown tongue edifieth himself; but he that prophesieth edifieth the church.

Romans 8:26 Likewise the Spirit also helpeth our infirmities: for we know not what we should pray for as we ought: but the Spirit itself maketh intercession for us with groanings which cannot be uttered.

v. 27 And he that searcheth the hearts knoweth what is the mind of the Spirit, because he maketh intercession for the saints according to the will of God.

Baptism by Fire

Matthew 3:12 Whose fan is in his hand, and he will thoroughly purge his floor, and gather his wheat into the garner; but he will burn up the chaff with unquenchable fire.

V. New Testament Examples

The Upper Room

Acts 2:1 And when the day of Pentecost was fully come, they were all with one accord in one place.

v. 2 And suddenly there came a sound from heaven as of a rushing mighty wind, and it filled all the house where they were sitting.

v. 3 And there appeared unto them cloven tongues like as of fire, and it sat upon each of them.

v. 4 And they were all filled with the Holy Ghost, and began to speak with other tongues, as the Spirit gave them utterance.

Philip in Samaria

Acts 8:14 Now when the apostles which were at Jerusalem heard that Samaria had received the word of God, they sent unto them Peter and John:

v. 15 Who, when they were come down, prayed for them, that they might receive the Holy Ghost:

v. 16 (For as yet he was fallen upon none of them: only they were baptized in the name of the Lord Jesus.)

v. 17 Then laid they their hands on them, and they received the Holy Ghost.

Paul

Acts 9:17 And Ananias went his way, and entered into the house; and putting his hands on him said, Brother Saul, the Lord, even Jesus, that appeared unto thee in the way as thou camest, hath sent me, that thou mightest receive thy sight, and be filled with the Holy Ghost.

Cornelius' Household

Acts 10:44 While Peter yet spake these words, the Holy Ghost fell on all them which heard the word.

v. 45. And they of the circumcision which believed were astonished, as many as came with Peter, because that on the Gentiles also was poured out the gift of the Holy Ghost.

v. 46 For they heard them speak with tongues, and magnify God. Then answered Peter,

v. 47 Can any man forbid water, that these should not be baptized, which have received the Holy Ghost as well as we?

v. 48 And he commanded them to be baptized in the name of the Lord. Then prayed they him to tarry certain days.

Believers in Ephesus

Acts 19:1 And it came to pass, that, while Apollos was at Corinth, Paul having passed through the upper coasts came to Ephesus: and finding certain disciples,

v. 2 He said unto them, Have ye received the Holy Ghost since ye believed? And they said unto him, We have not so much as heard whether there be any Holy Ghost.

v. 3 And he said unto them, Unto what then were ye baptized? And they said, Unto John's baptism.

v. 4 Then said Paul, John verily baptized with the baptism of repentance, saying unto the people, that they should believe on him which should come after him, that is, on Christ Jesus.

v. 5 When they heard this, they were baptized in the name of the Lord Jesus.

v. 6 And when Paul had laid his hands upon them, the Holy Ghost came on them; and they spake with tongues, and prophesied.

VI.   Introduction to Gifts of the Spirit

Nine Gifts in Three Categories

- Revelation Gifts
- Power Gifts
- Utterance Gifts

1 Corinthians 12:8 For to one is given by the Spirit the word of wisdom; to another the word of knowledge by the same Spirit;

v. 9 To another faith by the same Spirit; to another the gifts of healing by the same Spirit;

v. 10 To another the working of miracles; to another prophecy; to another discerning of spirits; to another divers kinds of tongues; to another the interpretation of tongues.

1 Corinthians 12:11 But all these worketh that one and the selfsame Spirit, dividing to every man severally as he will.

PLANK FIVE

Restoring Healing to the
Body of Christ

PLANK FIVE

Restoring Healing to the Body of Christ

Faith and Our Five Senses

Your natural senses have nothing to do with faith, and true faith must ignore them.

If you walk by faith, you cannot walk by sight. If you are to consider the Word of God as true, then you cannot always consider the evidences of your senses are true.

Feeling, smelling, tasting, hearing, and seeing are the senses by which the natural person is directed. The Word of God and faith are the two factors by which the spiritual person is directed.

The natural person walks by the senses, but the spiritual person walks by faith in the Word of God.

– T. L. Osborn[1]

Cancer, Cocaine or the Cross?

Our society is so full of despair and hopelessness concerning the sick and terminally ill that a book advising how to commit suicide was the number one selling hardcover book in the "advice" category on the *New York Times* Best Seller List in 1991![1]

In a medically progressive society, supposedly the best and brightest in the world, nearly 1,400,000 new cases of cancer were reported in 2005, including more than 170,000 new cases of lung cancer and more than 200,000 new cases of breast cancer.[3]

The devil is ravaging our bodies and taking our lives at a torrid pace that almost defies description!

With all the supposed "healing power" within the Body of Christ, with all the cries of "greater works than He did shall we do," more than 70,000,000 Americans have one or more forms of heart and blood vessel disease, and heart disease-related conditions caused more than 927,000 deaths in 2004.[4]

The devil is having a party with our pathetic, disease-racked bodies! He has stolen the health that Christ purchased for us at Calvary.

The bodies of teenagers and adults continue to be abused by alcohol, marijuana, PCP, "uppers," cocaine, crack, caffeine, sedatives, tranquilizers and sleeping pills, and narcotics such as heroin. In one survey, 19,500,000 Americans age 12 years or older were current users of illicit drugs in 2003.[5]

Add to these obvious physical abuses the more subtle killers such as stress, high blood pressure, and obesity, and the health of our nation seems weak and anemic.

We are living in a society where hospitals dot communities like schools, where there is an emergency room every three blocks, where thousands upon thousands of victims are lying on hospital beds, captive to some of the most fearsome diseases ever known to the human race.

While you are reading this book, thousands of people all over our cities are dying from incurable diseases. People are taking hair brushes and scratching their flesh trying to get away from the pain and the itching and the burning.

We do not like to think about such things.

We do not like to think that the little pain in our body – maybe in our hip or ankle – could herald the end of our lives. Finally, when we are brave enough to go to the doctor, he looks across the table at us and says, "You should have come sooner. Your bones are full of cancer."

We do not like to think that in less than two months all of our hair could be gone because of chemotherapy, and that a 180-pound frame could melt down to 105 pounds.

We do not like to think of the indignities of lying in a hospital and smelling the medicines and seeing the nursing staff run tubes in and out of bodies, sticking morphine in our bodies every two or three hours just to dull our senses enough to try and keep us comfortable until we die.

We do not like to think about AIDS. Oh, we like to preach about homosexuals; but where is our compassion for these men and women across this country? Where is our compassion for the innocent babies born with AIDS already in their system, babies that have no hope of living.

We are in the midst of an onslaught from hell called sickness and disease.

Satan has stolen the healing plank from our holy bridge!

While the church plays patty-cake and the religious world refines their denominational theory and expounds upon experiential theology, there are suffering, bleeding, hurting, and dying people in the world all around us. In all their exegesis, they are "x-ing" Jesus right out of their lives.

What About the Word?

The Bible says,

**"And Jesus went about all the cities and villages,
teaching in their synagogues, and preaching the gospel**

185

of the kingdom, and healing every sickness and every disease among the people.

"But when he saw the multitudes, he was moved with compassion on them, because they fainted, and were scattered abroad, as sheep having no shepherd."

Matthew 9:35-36

For seventeen years I grew up in a church – church attendance was not optional; yet, I never did see anyone get healed!

I saw seven members of my own family die. I despised the sight of the funeral home on the east side of Columbus. I used to write down the names of my family members who were dying to see if they were dying in alphabetical order and to see if I was next. As a little boy, I saw so many deaths that when I picked up my little puppy outside the house, I would say to him, "I used to love you; but I'm not going to love you anymore, because if I love you, then that means you will die."

If you have had any experiences similar to mine, then it certainly is no wonder that so many Christians have a huge, gaping hole in their holy bridge where divine healing used to be.

Once, the church had the truth of Calvary, the double cure, firmly nailed down. Today, we cannot believe for the healing of a headache!

How can religious traditionalists accept only half of the atonement?

How can so many church leaders accept salvation but reject divine healing.

What we have done is to equate our doctrine with our experience.

Cold religion looks at God's blueprint for the bridge of grace in 1 Peter 2:24:

"Who his own self bare our sins in his own body on the tree, that we, being dead to sins, should live unto righteousness: by whose stripes ye were healed."

They plainly see God's provision for healing of the human body. But then, as they look around at their overwhelming amount of sickness and disease and see an apparent absence of healing manifestations, their carnal logic reasons that since they do not see divine healing, therefore, it must not be for us today.

The devil has robbed our holy bridge of the foundational plank of divine healing and replaced it with an experiential theology that says, "I prayed for ten people; two of them got well, so that must mean God only wants to heal 20 percent of the time."

We do not serve a god of experiential theology.

Smith Wigglesworth once said, "I am not moved by what I see; I am moved by what I believe."

Regardless of what you are currently experiencing, the atonement of the cross of Christ is two-fold. It is vital that the church know this central fact, so I am going to share with you divine revelation on the subject of Calvary, the double cure.

Before you go on, I want you to do something for me: put out of your mind everything you have ever heard regarding divine healing!

Put all religious traditions out of your mind; put all the Christianese out of your mind. I want to take you down a path of Bible basics and build a foundation against which the gates of hell cannot prevail.

Two Cures, One Physician

Calvary was a double cure.

Number one, it saved you from an eternity spent in hell.

Number two, it healed your physical body.

That is the gospel of Jesus Christ.

"This gospel of the kingdom shall be preached in all the world for a witness unto all nations; and then shall the end come."

Matthew 24:14

The church has plenty of preaching. There are more Bible schools than in the history of the world. We have more Christian programs, more printed material, more books, more newsletters, more Christian education, more singing, and more gospel preaching than we have ever had in the history of the world.

On the first day of many Bible schools, students hear that God is one perfect, personal Spirit. But then, later in the semester, that same Bible school will teach that healing was for only a time, a special period, and that healing is not for today. Well, let me ask you, "How can a perfect God suddenly become less than perfect?" If He was perfect when He was healing, then He becomes less than perfect when He is not.

We are not hearing ALL of the gospel.

God was a healer in the Old Testament (Psalm 103:3; Exodus 15:26; Exodus 23:25).

God, through Jesus, obviously is a healer in the New Testament.

So where is it written that God is no longer a healer?

The Bible says that God cannot change, and that He heals our diseases.

The world does not need our creeds or denominational lingo. It is time we went back to preaching the old-fashioned, heartfelt, Holy Ghost, sin-eradicating, life-changing, body-healing gospel of Jesus Christ: Calvary, the double cure.

I get up in the morning and thank God that I am healed of cancer.

"Well, Pastor Parsley, I'm sorry to hear you have cancer."

I don't, and I didn't.

God healed me of it! I praise God for healing me of arthritis, headaches, and heart attacks. My Savior is abiding in me, continually, in the present tense, redeeming my body back from the devil!

It is time to put the plank of healing back in God's gospel bridge.

In Matthew 9, Jesus encountered the man sick of palsy. In verse 2, He told him that his sins were forgiven. In verse 6, Jesus told him to take up his bed and go home – he was healed. In verse 22, the woman with the issue of blood was healed. In verse 24, Jairus' daughter was raised from the dead. In verse 29, two blind men were healed. In verse 32, Jesus cast a devil out of a dumb man and he spoke. The multitudes that followed Jesus marveled and said, "It was never so seen in Israel."

But the Pharisees said, "He casteth out devils through the prince of the devils." The religious crowd always has an argument against anything spiritual.

Jesus did not debate with these men.

Instead, he continued to minister.

> **"And Jesus went about all the cities and villages teaching in their synagogues, and preaching the gospel of the kingdom, and healing every sickness and every disease among the people.**
>
> **"But when he saw the multitudes, he was moved with compassion on them..."**
>
> **Matthew 9:35-36**

Notice, the Bible does not say He was moved with sympathy. Compassion surpasses sympathy. Sympathy says, "Isn't that too bad?" Compassion says, "I want to do something about your problem."

I once took a survey of the thousands of people gathered in one of our services at World Harvest Church in Columbus, Ohio. I asked the people present that had some form of malady, malfunction, infirmity, sickness, or disease in their body to stand.

"If everything in your body is not functioning absolutely perfectly," I challenged them," then stand on your feet."

At least 95 percent of the congregation stood. In the city of Columbus, Ohio, there are more than 700,000 people. Just think how many of those people are sick!

We have programmed ourselves that if we get cancer we had better unloose the Word of God and the anointing of God to get rid of it. Yet, we put up with sinus problems, flu symptoms, earaches, infections, backaches, neck aches, and non-cancerous tumors.

The Bible says that Jesus healed them all! Think of the thousands of people He must have healed. Do you realize that every one of those sick people had some form of pain, weakness, infirmity, malady, malfunction, disease, or distress?

Yet, Jesus preached the gospel of the kingdom and healed them all.

"That's fine for Jesus. He was the Son of God. You will never be Jesus. You're a prune pit!"

Jesus lives in me, and He tells me in John 14:12 that I am commissioned to do the works He did – and even greater!

Today, His Spirit lives inside of you.

Jesus was not a joker or a kidder when it came to important doctrines, so I believe He really meant it when he declared,

> **"Behold, I give unto you power to tread on serpents and scorpions, and over all the power of the enemy: and nothing shall by any means hurt you."**
>
> **Luke 10:19**

If that is true, why is sickness still sapping the lives of our saints?

Get this foundational truth in your spirit: Divine healing belongs to you today, because God never changes.

The last verse of the gospel of John maintains that if every-thing Jesus did in His three and one-half years of earthy ministry were recorded **"that even the world itself could not contain the books that should be written."**

Now, please realize today we do not have everything recorded that Jesus did. He did so much more! We have only a condensed version of what He did, but it is enough for us.

John also said in his gospel that what He did record was writ-ten **"...that ye might believe that Jesus is the Christ, the Son of God; and that believing ye might have life through his name"** (John 20:31).

> **"All scripture is given by inspiration of God, and is profitable for doctrine..."**
>
> **2 Timothy 3:16**

God has made a way for you to cross over the bridge from sickness to perfect health.

Jesus said, "I looked at the multitude, and I had compassion." Jesus bridged the hopeless gap with His own body on the tree.

Visit any hospital. You will see people sitting in waiting rooms weeping and crying, wondering if at any minute the doctor will come out of the operating room and tell them, "Your loved one did not make it." You will see babies born with birth defects, with heads swollen larger than their shoulders, and children with twisted, crippled limbs.

In any hospital in America, there are people waiting to hear the gospel of the kingdom, people who need to know the One who paid the price to heal them.

It is time for the Body of Christ to be moved with compassion and minister to the multitudes. We must see them hurting, bleed-ing, and dying without Jesus as Savior and Healer. When are we going to see our preachers going to the multitudes? When are we going to care more about the hurting, depressed, dying, diseased, destitute, and depraved human race than we do the race for gospel politics?

Jesus healed *every* sickness and disease.

This is good news.

He can heal the cancer patients, people with crippling arthritis, and Alzheimer's disease. Somewhere outside the city of Jerusalem on a lonely hillside, a man was crucified; and by His stripes we were healed.

Jesus was moved with compassion **"...because they fainted, and were scattered abroad, as sheep having no shepherd" (Matthew 9:36).** The shepherds are returning – shepherds to lead the sheep into green pastures.

The modern-day shepherd needs to lead the sheep away from poison grass on the path to righteousness for His name's sake.

Let me take you by the hand and lead you into green pastures where you can eat and be filled, where you can prosper and be healed.

> **"Beware lest any man spoil you through philosophy and vain deceit, after the tradition of men, after the rudiments of the world, and not after Christ."**
>
> **Colossians 2:8**

I believe it is time we went back to the full gospel. I believe it is time we announce, like heralds, "Jesus is our healer!"

The Key Question

What is the number one question concerning divine healing?

Is it whether or not Jesus has the power to heal you?

No, because in Mark 9:23 Jesus says, **"If thou canst believe, all things are possible to him that believeth."** He is telling you, "It is not a question of what *I* can do; but rather, it is a question of what *you* can believe."

There are nineteen miraculous healings recorded in Matthew, Mark, Luke, and John; every one of them has tremendous significance for us. Out of the vast multitudes that Jesus healed, God picked out nineteen to put in His Book. I believe He wants to teach us something from each one of them.

Is the number one question concerning divine healing, "Can I receive my healing?"

No, I do not believe that is it either. Can you honestly believe that when someone is sick they may not want to get well?

The number one question of humanity surrounding the subject of divine healing seems to be, "Does Jesus really heal today?"

That question is clearly answered by God's Word. Jesus healed in Matthew, Mark, Luke, and John; and the book of Hebrews says He is **"the same yesterday, and to day, and for ever" (Hebrews 13:8).**

So what is the REAL question concerning divine healing? I believe we find it in Mark 1:40-44:

"And there came a leper to him, beseeching him, and kneeling down to him, and saying unto him, If thou wilt, thou canst make me clean. And Jesus, moved with compassion, put forth his hand, and touched him, and saith unto him, I will; be thou clean.

"And as soon as he had spoken, immediately the leprosy departed from him, and he was cleansed.

"And he straitly charged him, and forthwith sent him away;

"And saith unto him, See thou say nothing to any man: but go thy way, show thyself to the priest, and offer for thy cleansing those things which Moses commanded, for a testimony unto them."

The reason I do not believe the number one question concerning divine healing today is whether or not Jesus has the power to heal is because I believe the Bible.

If you believe the Bible, you *know* Jesus has the power to heal. Jesus has power to stop your bleeding, for He stopped the woman's issue of blood. He has power to wipe blindness out of your eyes, for He wiped the blindness out of Bartimaeus' eyes. He has the power to unstop your deaf ears, for He unstopped the ears of the deaf. He healed the paralyzed man in Matthew 9; Jesus has the power today to straighten out your crooked limbs.

He scattered the stars in the heavens, traced places for the rivers to flow, put oceans in their boundaries and spun the world upside down and commanded that they not pass over. He cast the legion of demons out of the demoniac of Gadera.

Jesus has the power to do it: the power to save, to heal, to deliver.

To most Christians, the problem is the same problems this man had in Mark 1:40. Throughout the entirety of the Word of God, as far as I can tell, this is the only instance where the will of God to heal was questioned. It seems that back in Bible days they had no question in their minds concerning God's will to heal.

The religious people of Jesus' day had no problem with Jesus healing the man sick of the palsy (Matthew 9, Mark 2). What they balked at was that Jesus had power to forgive sin.

Today, religious opinion has come full circle. The religious world has no problem with the fact that Jesus can and will forgive sins, but they strongly question His will to heal. A literal reading of this scripture in Mark 2:9 could sound like this: "It's no easier for Me to save than to heal; and it's no easier for Me to heal than to save."

In only one out of nineteen instances is there ever anyone that is recorded that questioned the will of God to heal. The man said, **"If thou wilt, thou canst make me clean."**

It is unfortunate, but he is the primary example of the New Testament church today. We do not question God's power to heal. The number one question we ask is, "Does God really will to heal us?"

Forget Paul's Thorn!

We know God has the power to heal. He translated us out of the power of darkness and into the kingdom of light. He caused us to see spiritually when we were blind, passed us from death to life, washed away our sins.

We know He has the power. He is coming on clouds of glory and great power.

You know Jesus has the *power* to heal. In this chapter, I am absolutely intent on convincing you that not only does He have the power to heal you, it is His absolute and perfect will to heal you. We do not have to sift through Paul's thorn, Job's boils, or Timothy's sick stomach to try to understand the perfect will of God.

You must realize Paul's infirmity was not in his flesh; it was his soulish man – his mind, will, and emotions. We know this because he told us the thorn was a messenger of Satan sent to buffet him. Paul tells us that when he prayed, the answer he received about this was **"My grace is sufficient for thee…" (2 Corinthians 12:9).**

What does that mean?

"Grace" means the availability of God's power to deliver. Jesus said to Paul, "The availability of God's power to deliver you is sufficient to meet any need you might have."

It is time preachers stop trying to make excuses for their lack of faith and understanding of the Word of God. Do not tell me that God puts cancer on people to teach them something!

That is a lie that comes from the smoky pit of hell. You cannot find that in the Bible. You cannot substantiate that with the Word of God.

I am tired of preachers that have the audacity to tell people that God put AIDS on them and God put cancer on them and God put arthritis on them.

If God put cancer or arthritis on you, He would have to steal it from the devil.

Sickness does not belong to God!

John 10:10 says, **"The thief cometh not, but for to steal, and to kill, and to destroy: I am come that they might have life, and that they might have it more abundantly.**

Paul's thorn was in his soulish man and came because of abundant revelation. Most of us do not qualify for what Paul received. The thorn in the flesh is a messenger of Satan sent to Paul because of his abundant revelation. Paul qualified. He said, "I knew a man fourteen years ago caught up into the third heaven." Paul said he was caught up into the third heaven, into the throne of God, and heard things not lawful for a man to utter.

When you get to the point where you cannot tell whether you are in the Spirit or in the flesh, when you are standing at the throne of Almighty God, when your abundant revelations are so excessive that the devil assigns a messenger just to buffet you, then you can talk about the thorn in your flesh. But do not go telling me that little aching pain in your body is your thorn in the flesh.

Jesus came to seek and to save that which was lost; **"... [He] went about doing good, and healing all that were oppressed of the devil..." (Acts 10:38).**

Others claim, "Jesus put me in a hospital to be a witness for Him."

Well, if that's the case, then yank those tubes right out of your body! Tell the nurse not to put that medicine in your mouth. IF Jesus put you there, you had better stay put, stay right where He put you. If He wants you sick, why are you trying so hard to get well?

I have noticed something about hospitals. They have an entrance for visitors. God does not have to make you sick for you to get in.

We need to preach the gospel of the kingdom and not some other gospel, not some man-made, traditional gospel. The man in Mark 1:40 had no problem receiving divine healing once he knew what the will of God was for his life.

Do Not Waver

"If any of you lack wisdom, let him ask of God, that giveth to all men liberally, and upbraideth not; and it shall be given him. But let him ask in faith, nothing wavering. For he that wavereth is like a wave of the sea driven with the wind and tossed."

James 1:5-6

Faith begins where the will of God is known!

If there is a question in your mind concerning the will of God to heal you, you cannot get over into the arena of faith; and **"Without faith, it is impossible to please him..." (Hebrews 11:6)**.

Over and over again in those nineteen instances of healing, Jesus said, "Be it done unto you according to your faith." Faith is the steadfast confidence, trust, and assurance that what God has promised, He is able to perform.

God wants to build up a group of believers who absolutely know the will, the plan, the purpose, the desire, and the directive of their God. I think it is a sad indictment on the Body of Christ that we have Bible schools all over America and men and women with Ph.D.'s and other degrees; and yet, we cannot find the will of God.

All you need to know for the will of God is the prayer of the Apostle in 3 John 2:

"Beloved, I wish above all things that thou mayest prosper and be in health, even as thy soul prospereth."

You say, "I have this sickness to teach me something."

That is a lie. Let me ask you a question: "If it were true that God put sickness and disease, pain, and infirmity on us to teach us something, wouldn't there be at least one verse of scripture in all the Bible to tell us so?

Well, where is it?

Where is that Matthew, Mark, Luke, or John example where someone came to Jesus and asked for healing, and He said, "No, the Father is going to leave this sickness on you. He's working a purpose in you; and He has to teach you something. And Jesus went His way, and there was great rejoicing?"

There is not one verse like that in the entire Bible!

Let us look for a scripture example. How about Mark 1:40,41?

> **"...If thou wilt, thou canst make me clean. And Je-sus...saith unto him, I will: be thou clean."**

> **"The anointing which ye have received of him abideth in you, and ye need not that any man teach you..."**
>
> **1 John 2:27**

You have no need that any man should teach you, but that the Spirit of God should teach you.

It is the Holy Spirit's responsibility to lead you into all truth.

> **"Howbeit when he, the Spirit of truth, is come, he will guide you into all truth: for he shall not speak of himself; but whatsoever he shall hear, that shall he speak: and he will show you things to come."**
>
> **John 16:13**

God *never* gave the right to teach His children sickness and disease, cancer and infirmity, birth defects or AIDS.

The number one question concerning divine healing is not, "Does God have power to heal?" It is "Is it God's will to heal me?"

Once you understand that healing is God's will for your life, then you can lock your faith on His desire for you.

God Does Not Lie!

The Body of Christ needs to repent today. I am calling the Body of Christ to repentance for calling God a liar. The real question that you are asking is not, "Is it God's will to heal me?" The real question you are asking is, "Is God a liar?"

"Why, no," you say. "I'd never call God a liar." Then do not let that sickness and disease stay in your body.

I know this sounds harsh, but I am angry with the devil. You are hurting, suffering, with pain in your body. I am angry with the preachers who tell you that it is God's will for that hurt to stay there.

For God, there is only one will concerning your healing, and that is His will to heal you, to take that pain out of your body, to curse every cancer cell and replace it with a living, life-giving cell by the power of God.

"If it were not God's will to heal you, He shouldn't have!" That thought just exploded in my spirit one morning as I lay prostrate with the Bible open in front of me, reading Isaiah 53:4-5 and 1 Peter 2:24. God spoke to my spirit and said, "If it was not My will to heal them, then I should not have done it."

Healing is not a promise; healing is a fact.

Isaiah 53:5 declares,

"But he was wounded for our transgressions, he was bruised for our iniquities: the chastisement of our peace was upon him; and with his stripes we are healed."

At Calvary, there was a great healing transfer where the responsibility for healing was switched from God to you.

The power to heal has been transferred to YOU! Jesus is the One asking you, "Is it YOUR will to be healed?"

In John 5, Jesus was at the pool of Bethesda. There was a man lying there; he had been lying there for years. Jesus said to the man, "Wilt thou be made whole?" What Jesus really said was, "Are you serious about being healed?"

"He sent his word, and healed them…"

Psalm 107:20

Do you have a Bible? If you have one, you are already healed, for His Word on healing was sent from God to you.

Healing is a fact, not a promise. It says, **"He sent his word, and healed them."** If you have the Word, you have been healed.

Almost 2,000 years ago, the Roman centurion at the flogging post took out a whip and began to beat the back of Jesus until the flesh was ripped from His bones. Every drop of blood shed in Pilate's Hall was not just for your salvation; it was also for the divine healing of your body.

When we come together and take communion, Jesus says, "As often as you eat this bread, remember this: This is My body which has been broken for the healing of your body. Eat of it." (Matthew 26:26; 1 Corinthians 11:26; Mark 14:22; Luke 22:19.)

Healing is the children's bread. Eat of that healing. It belongs to you. It is yours. God's will is to heal you.

Isaiah 53:4 says that Jesus has already suffered the punishment for our sickness and borne as a penalty all our pain. If it was not God's will to heal you, He shouldn't have, because healing is not a promise; it is an accomplished fact.

You are healed. You have been made whole from the top of your head to the soles of your feet. Faith begins where the will of God is known.

In Luke 13, not only did Jesus prove it was His will for you to be healed, He proved He would stand up and fight in the face of every opposing force to secure your right to receive that healing.

In this scripture, a woman had been bent over for eighteen years. Jesus came into the synagogue and spoke to her. He said, "I have the answer. I'm the Savior; I'm the Healer."

The woman had been bent over and bowed down for eighteen years!

Notice what Jesus said. He said, **"Woman, thou art loosed from thine infirmity" (Luke 13:12).**

In the natural, she was not released. She was still bent down. But Jesus reached into the Spirit realm and brought back her healing. Jesus no more put sickness on her to teach her something than

He put sin on you to teach you something. Jesus died to deliver you and rose again to see to it that you received the message.

Millions are bent down, hurting, bruised, battered, bleeding, destitute, and with no hope. Do you realize right now there are people in such excruciating pain that they feel if they do not get relief they will go out of their minds? The doctors know how to shoot pain medication in them.

God is not offering a numbing – He is offering deliverance! It is God's will to set you free; to take those cancer cells out of your body; to release you from the dark, aching, cold pain of that arthritic condition; to deliver your mother or father from Alzheimer's disease; to deliver your child from that birth defect.

Faith begins when the will of God is known.

The woman was bent over, helpless, and hopeless; but Jesus said, **"Woman, thou art loosed from thine infirmity."**

Hear what the religious people said. They said,

> **"...There are six days in which men ought to work: in them therefore come and be healed, and not on the sabbath day."**
>
> **Luke 13:14**

How would they know anyway? No one was ever healed in their services! This is the Sabbath day! Jesus stood up and fought for her right to be healed, just like He will stand up and fight for you today.

He replied, **"Ought not this woman, being a daughter of Abraham, whom Satan hath bound, lo, these eighteen years, be loosed from this bond on the sabbath day?"** (Luke 13:16).

The Bible goes on to say, **"And when he had said these things, all his adversaries were ashamed: and all the people rejoiced for all the glorious things that were done by him"** (Luke 13:17).

Let us get back to Bible basics. Let us look religious tradition right in the eye and declare that Jesus is our Savior, and Jesus is our Healer!

The next time you experience pain, pray this prayer: "Lord Jesus, I believe you carried my sins to Calvary. I am not bound to those sins; You washed them away. Your Word promises me that not only did Your blood cover my sins, but You carried my sicknesses and my pain to the cross with You. I look to the cross. I believe with all my heart this back pain (or whatever the illness) I am experiencing now was laid on You at Calvary; and by faith, right now, I believe in the substitutionary act of Jesus. He took this pain from me."

In praying this way, you are making a confession. You cannot be saved without expressing that Jesus was your substitute and that He carried your sins away.

Look to Jesus that exact same way for your healing. The same blood that washed away your sins took that pain out of your back.

The same blood.

It is your covenant right.

Pray, "Jesus, You took this pain; You bore this hurt on the cross so I no longer have to bear it. You carried it to the cross. Lord, thank You."

Once you confess the promise out loud, then put your faith into action.

Jesus bore every disease – AIDS, headaches, backaches, cancer, liver disease – they were all laid upon Him so you did not have to carry them.

If you can believe God that the blood of Jesus Christ provided your eternal salvation, then you have no other conscientious, justifiable, correct conclusion to draw except that the same blood provided freedom from every sickness and disease and pain that humanity has or ever will suffer.

Healing is in the blood.

On that crucifixion day, which Isaiah saw so vividly, the Son of God willingly endured the flesh-tearing strokes of a Roman whip across His back. With each blood-letting incision, Jesus bore upon Himself the nauseating agony of every disease mankind would ever know.

He suffered through the intense torment of those lashes so we could proclaim, "By His stripes we are healed!"

Jesus became our substitute. He suffered and died in our place.

Today, you are cleansed from your unrighteousness and all manner of sickness.

The apostle Peter declared,

> **"...Christ also suffered for us...Who his own self bare our sins in his own body on the tree, that we, being dead to sins, should live unto righteousness: by whose stripes ye were healed."**
>
> **1 Peter 2:21, 24**

Endnotes

[1] T.L. Osborn, *Healing the Sick* (Tulsa: Harrison House, 1986), p. 119.

[2] *New York Times.*, 18 August 1991.

[3] "Cancer: Estimated New Cases (2005) and Survival Rates in the U.S.." Infoplease. © 2000–2006 Pearson Education, publishing as Infoplease. 25 Apr. 2006 <http://www.infoplease.com/ipa/A0883543.html>. (April 25, 2006).

[4] Thomas Thom, Nancy Haase, Wayne Rosamond, Virginia J. Howard, John Rumsfeld, Teri Manolio, Zhi-Jie Zheng, Katherine Flegal, Christopher O'Donnell, Steven Kittner, Donald Lloyd-Jones, David C. Goff, Jr., Yuling Hong, Members of the Statistics Committee and Stroke Statistics Subcommittee, Robert Adams, Gary Friday, Karen Furie, Philip Gorelick, Brett Kissela, John Marler, James Meigs, Veronique Roger, Stephen Sidney, Paul Sorlie, Julia Steinberger, Sylvia Wasserthiel-Smoller, Matthew Wilson, and Philip Wolf. "Heart Disease and Stroke Statistics—2006 Update: A report From the American Heart Association Statistics Committee and Stroke Statistics Subcommittee." Circulation 2006 Feb 14;113(6):e85-151. Epub 2006 Jan 11.
<http://circ.ahajournals.org/cgi/content/short/113/6/e85> (April 25, 2006).

[5] "Overview of Drug Use in the United States." Infoplease. © 2000–2006 Pearson Education, publishing as Infoplease. 25 Apr. 2006.
<http://www.infoplease.com/ipa/A0880105.html>. (April 25, 2006).

Your Healing Tool Kit

Here Are the Tools, the Spiritual Hammer and Nails, You Need to Biblically Repair and Restore the Healing Plank in Your Life.

I.   Healing Under the Old Covenant

Healing of Plague

Numbers 16:50   And Aaron returned unto Moses unto the door of the tabernacle of the congregation: and the plague was stayed.

Healing of Leprosy

2 Kings 5:10   And Elisha sent a messenger unto him, saying, Go and wash in Jordan seven times, and thy flesh shall come again to thee, and thou shalt be clean.

v. 11   But Naaman was wroth, and went away, and said, Behold, I thought, He will surely come out to me, and stand, and call on the name of the Lord his God, and strike his hand over the place, and recover the leper.

v. 12   Are not Abana and Pharpar, rivers of Damascus, better than all the waters of Israel? may I not wash in them, and be clean? So he turned and went away in a rage.

v. 13   And his servants came near, and spake unto him, and said, My father, if the prophet had bid thee do some great thing, wouldest thou not have done it? how much rather then, when he saith to thee, Wash, and be clean?

v. 14 Then went he down, and dipped himself seven times in Jordan, according to the saying of the man of God: and his flesh came again like unto the flesh of a little child, and he was clean.

Healing of Palsy

1 Kings 13:6 And the king answered and said unto the man of God, Intreat now the face of the Lord thy God, and pray for me, that my hand may be restored me again. And the man of God besought the Lord, and the king's hand was restored him again, and became as it was before.

Healed of Snake Bite

Numbers 21:8 And the Lord said unto Moses, Make thee a fiery serpent, and set it upon a pole: and it shall come to pass, that every one that is bitten, when he looketh upon it, shall live.

v. 9 And Moses made a serpent of brass, and put it upon a pole, and it came to pass, that if a serpent had bitten any man, when he beheld the serpent of brass, he lived.

Raised From the Dead

1 King 17:19 And he said unto her, Give me thy son. And he took him out of her bosom, and carried him up into a loft, where he abode, and laid him upon his own bed.

v. 20 And he cried unto the Lord, and said, O Lord my God, hast thou also brought evil upon the widow with whom I sojourn, by slaying her son?

v. 21 And he stretched himself upon the child three times, and cried unto the Lord, and said, O Lord my God, I pray thee, let this child's soul come into him again.

v. 22 And the Lord heard the voice of Elijah; and the soul of the child came into him again, and he revived.

v. 23 And Elijah took the child, and brought him down out of the chamber into the house, and delivered him unto his mother: and Elijah said, See, thy son liveth.

2 Kings 4:32 And when Elisha was come into the house, behold, the child was dead, and laid upon his bed.

v. 33 He went in therefore, and shut the door upon them twain, and prayed unto the Lord.

v. 34 And he went up, and lay upon the child, and put his mouth upon his mouth, and his eyes upon his eyes, and his hands upon his hands: and he stretched himself upon the child; and the flesh of the child waxed warm.

v. 35 Then he returned, and walked in the house to and fro; and went up, and stretched himself upon him: and the child sneezed seven times, and the child opened his eyes.

v. 36 And he called Gehazi, and said, Call this Shunammite. So he called her. And when she was come in unto him, he said, Take up thy son.

v. 37 Then she went in, and fell at his feet, and bowed herself to the ground, and took up her son, and went out.

2 Kings 8:4 And the king talked with Gehazi the servant of the man of God, saying, Tell me, I pray thee, all the great things that Elisha hath done.

v. 5 And it came to pass, as he was telling the king how he had restored a dead body to life, that, behold, the woman, whose son he had restored to life, cried to the king for her house and for her land. And Gehazi said, My lord, O king, this is the woman, and this is her son, whom Elisha restored to life.

II.   Healing Under the New Covenant

Leprosy Healed

Matthew 8:2 And, behold, there came a leper and worshipped him, saying, Lord, if thou wilt, thou canst make me clean.

v. 3 And Jesus put forth his hand, and touched him, saying, I will; be thou clean. And immediately his leprosy was cleansed.

Mark 1:40 And there came a leper to him, beseeching him, and kneeling down to him, and saying unto him, If thou wilt, thou canst make me clean.

v. 41 And Jesus, moved with compassion, put forth his hand, and touched him, and saith unto him, I will; be thou clean.

v. 42 And as soon as he had spoken, immediately the leprosy departed from him, and he was cleansed.

Luke 5:12 And it came to pass, when he was in a certain city, behold a man full of leprosy: who seeing Jesus fell on his face, and besought him, saying, Lord, if thou wilt, thou canst make me clean.

v. 13 And he put forth his hand, and touched him, saying, I will: be thou clean. And immediately the leprosy departed from him.

v. 14 And he charged him to tell no man: but go, and show thyself to the priest, and offer for thy cleansing, according as Moses commanded, for a testimony unto them.

Palsy Healed

Matthew 9:2 And, behold, they brought to him a man sick of the palsy, lying on a bed: and Jesus seeing their faith said unto the sick of the palsy; Son, be of good cheer; thy sins be forgiven thee.

v. 3 And, behold, certain of the scribes said within themselves, This man blasphemeth.

v. 4 And Jesus knowing their thoughts said, Wherefore think ye evil in your hearts?

v. 5 For whether is easier, to say, Thy sins be forgiven thee; or to say, Arise, and walk?

v. 6 But that ye may know that the Son of man hath power on earth to forgive sins, (then saith he to the sick of the palsy,) Arise, take up thy bed, and go unto thine house.

v. 7 And he arose, and departed to his house.

Mark 2:11 I say unto thee, Arise, and take up thy bed, and go thy way into thine house.

v. 12 And immediately he arose, took up the bed, and went forth before them all; insomuch that they were all amazed, and glorified God, saying, We never saw it on this fashion.

Luke 5:21 And the scribes and the Pharisees began to reason, saying, Who is this which speaketh blasphemies? Who can forgive sins, but God alone?

v. 22 But when Jesus perceived their thoughts, he answering said unto them, What reason ye in your hearts?

v. 23 Whether is easier, to say, Thy sins be forgiven thee; or to say, Rise up and walk?

v. 24 But that ye may know that the Son of man hath power upon earth to forgive sins, (he said unto the sick of the palsy,) I say unto thee, Arise, and take up thy couch, and go into thine house.

v. 25 And immediately he rose up before them, and took up that whereon he lay, and departed to his own house, glorifying God.

Fever Healed

Matthew 8:14 And when Jesus was come into Peter's house, he saw his wife's mother laid, and sick of a fever.

v. 15 And he touched her hand, and the fever left her: and she arose, and ministered unto them.

Mark 1:29 And forthwith, when they were come out of the synagogue, they entered into the house of Simon and Andrew, with James and John.

v. 30 But Simon's wife's mother lay sick of a fever, and anon they tell him of her.

v. 31 And he came and took her by the hand, and lifted her up; and immediately the fever left her, and she ministered unto them.

Luke 4:38 And he arose out of the synagogue, and entered into Simon's house. And Simon's wife's mother was taken with a great fever; and they besought him for her.

v. 39 And he stood over her, and rebuked the fever; and it left her: and immediately she arose and ministered unto them.

John 4:50 Jesus saith unto him, Go thy way; thy son liveth. And the man believed the word that Jesus had spoken unto him, and he went his way.

v. 51 And as he was now going down, his servants met him, and told him, saying, Thy son liveth.

v. 52 Then inquired he of them the hour when he began to amend. And they said unto him, Yesterday at the seventh hour the fever left him.

v. 53 So the father knew that it was at the same hour, in the which Jesus said unto him, Thy son liveth: and himself believed, and his whole house.

v. 54 This is again the second miracle that Jesus did, when he was come out of Judaea into Galilee.

Healed of Snake Bite

Acts 28:2 And the barbarous people showed us no little kindness: for they kindled a fire, and received us every one, because of the present rain, and because of the cold.

v. 3 And when Paul had gathered a bundle of sticks, and laid them on the fire, there came a viper out of the heat, and fastened on his hand.

v. 4   And when the barbarians saw the venomous beast hang on his hand, they said among themselves, No doubt this man is a murderer, whom, though he hath escaped the sea, yet vengeance suffereth not to live.

v. 5   And he shook off the beast into the fire, and felt no harm.

v. 6   Howbeit they looked when he should have swollen, or fallen down dead suddenly: but after they had looked a great while, and saw no harm come to him, they changed their minds, and said that he was a god.

Raised From the Dead

Matthew 9:24   He said unto them, Give place: for the maid is not dead, but sleepeth. And they laughed him to scorn.

v. 25   But when the people were put forth, he went in, and took her by the hand, and the maid arose.

Mark 5:22   And, behold, there cometh one of the rulers of the synagogue, Jairus by name; and when he saw him, he fell at his feet,

v. 23   And besought him greatly, saying, My little daughter lieth at the point of death: I pray thee, come and lay thy hands on her, that she may be healed; and she shall live.

v. 24   And Jesus went with him; and much people followed him, and thronged him.

v. 35   While he yet spake, there came from the ruler of the synagogue's house certain which said, Thy daughter is dead: why troublest thou the Master any further?

v. 36 As soon as Jesus heard the word that was spoken, he saith unto the ruler of the synagogue, Be not afraid, only believe.

v. 37 And he suffered no man to follow him, save Peter, and James, and John the brother of James.

v. 38 And he cometh to the house of the ruler of the synagogue, and seeth the tumult, and them that wept and wailed greatly.

v. 39 And when he was come in, he saith unto them, Why make ye this ado, and weep? the damsel is not dead, but sleepeth.

v. 40 And they laughed him to scorn. But when he had put them all out, he taketh the father and the mother of the damsel, and them that were with him, and entereth in where the damsel was lying.

v. 41 And he took the damsel by the hand, and said unto her, Talitha cumi; which is, being interpreted, Damsel, I say unto thee, arise.

v. 42 And straightway the damsel arose, and walked; for she was of the age of twelve years. And they were astonished with a great astonishment.

Luke 7:12 Now when he came nigh to the gate of the city, behold, there was a dead man carried out, the only son of his mother, and she was a widow: and much people of the city was with her.

v. 13 And when the Lord saw her, he had compassion on her, and said unto her, Weep not.

v. 14 And he came and touched the bier: and they that bare him stood still. And he said, Young man, I say unto thee, Arise.

v. 15 And he that was dead sat up, and began to speak. And he delivered him to his mother.

Luke 8:41 And, behold, there came a man named Jairus, and he was a ruler of the synagogue: and he fell down at Jesus' feet, and besought him that he would come into his house:

v. 42 For he had one only daughter, about twelve years of age, and she lay a dying. But as he went the people thronged him.

v. 43 And a woman having an issue of blood twelve years, which had spent all her living upon physicians, neither could be healed of any,

v. 44 Came behind him, and touched the border of his garment: and immediately her issue of blood stanched.

v. 45 And Jesus said, Who touched me? When all denied, Peter and they that were with him said, Master, the multitude throng thee and press thee, and sayest thou, Who touched me?

v. 46 And Jesus said, Somebody hath touched me: for I perceive that virtue is gone out of me.

v. 47 And when the woman saw that she was not hid, she came trembling, and falling down before him, she declared unto him before all the people for what cause she had touched him and how she was healed immediately.

v. 48 And he said unto her, Daughter, be of good comfort: thy faith hath made thee whole; go in peace.

v. 49 While he yet spake, there cometh one from the ruler of the synagogue's house, saying to him, Thy daughter is dead; trouble not the Master.

v. 50 But when Jesus heard it, he answered him, saying, Fear not: believe only, and she shall be made whole.

v. 51 And when he came into the house, he suffered no man to go in, save Peter, and James, and John, and the father and the mother of the maiden.

v. 52 And all wept, and bewailed her: but he said, Weep not; she is not dead, but sleepeth.

v. 53 And they laughed him to scorn, knowing that she was dead.

v. 54 And he put them all out, and took her by the hand, and called, saying, Maid, arise.

v. 55 And her spirit came again, and she arose straightway: and he commanded to give her meat.

John 11:43 And when he thus had spoken, he cried with a loud voice, Lazarus, come forth.

v. 44 And he that was dead came forth, bound hand and foot with graveclothes: and his face was bound about with a napkin. Jesus saith unto them, Loose him, and let him go.

John 12:9 Much people of the Jews therefore knew that he was there: and they came not for Jesus' sake only, but that they might see Lazarus also, whom he had raised from the dead.

PLANK SIX

**Restoring Financial Freedom
to the Body of Christ**

PLANK SIX

Restoring Financial Freedom to the Body of Christ

Love Has Never Yet Made a Sacrifice

(Does) that husband of yours have to keep telling you that he loves you, he loves you?...

Love is something you do. It isn't continually saying, "I'm doing this because I love you. I'm sacrificing because I love you. I'm giving because I love you."

He doesn't have to. You know in your own heart that he's doing it because he loves you.

Why in the world do you think Papa ate Mama's burnt cookies, and sat there and said, "Emma, these cookies are so good?"

I'm going to tell you something – the neighbor's dog wouldn't have eaten those burnt cookies, but Papa loved Mama. Mama wasn't a very good cook. I don't think she'd mind if I tell you that Mama wasn't a good cook. She was never a slave to her kitchen.

And yet Papa would say, "Oh, Emma, I would rather eat your food than Belle's best cooking, or the best dinner in the restaurant."

It wasn't Mama's good cooking. It was just because Papa loved Mama. And some of you wives can put the best meal in the world on the table, and if your husband doesn't like you I dare say he doesn't even know what he's eating, but he sits down at the table and eats your wonderful cooking.

There's something about love. Everybody's talking about it, but yet, you have to go to the Word of God to really analyze love, break it apart, and see what it's made of.

Love that talks of loving is not love, and so it is with your love for the Master. (Also I wonder) when somebody has to constantly tell you how much they love the Lord – "Oh, I love Him. Oh, I love the Lord." You don't have to tell the whole world how much you love Him. Your actions will speak louder than your words. It's the deeds you do. It's your everyday living.

It's a sacrifice you make for the Lord – and yet – love knows no such thing as a sacrifice. Not really. That word "sacrifice" will never be in your vocabulary. It will be taken out completely when you love the Lord enough. *Your giving will never be a sacrifice, never.*

When somebody comes and says, "Here's a gift, use it for the Lord's work, and I only wish it were more," I know love prompts the giving of that gift.

When somebody says, "Here is a real sacrificial gift, I hope you appreciate it," maybe they're giving it because they're propositioning God or something like that. You know good and well love isn't prompting the giving of that gift.

But when you can give and say, "I wish it were more. It's all that I have. It's the best that I have," God knows your heart.

When you can say, "I wish there was more strength in my body with which to serve Him. I wish I could do more for Him. I've done so little. I wish there was more that my hands could do. I wish I could give more than I'm giving," that is love!

But when you have to speak of your love, it is not love at all, for the Word of God says, "Love vaunteth not itself."

— Excerpts from a
radio message by
Kathryn Kuhlman[1]

Opening the Sealed Windows of Heaven

Did God goof?

Did He put too many people on too small a planet and leave too little in resources to take care of them all?

Hardly.

This world is FULL of wealth! The United States alone has a holding of gold that is valued at approximately $162.7 billion.[2] The current available silver in the world is estimated at a value of $5.85 trillion.[3] Coal is the nation's most abundant fossil fuel with an estimated 500 billion short tons currently in reserves.[4]

There is so much money printed in America that 150 billion dollars in U.S. currency is currently unaccounted for.[5] There are more than 2,250,000 millionaires living in America today.[6]

In a world of supposedly scant resources, there are literally TONS of almost every type of material for every man, woman, and child on the earth.

There is an abundance of wealth in the world; and it is yours for the taking, for the gospel of Jesus Christ.

But the devil has blinded the eyes of Christians and attempted to give them a poverty mentality.

He gets you to focus on the famines in foreign countries, where people are starving.

They are starving, but not because God did not provide more than enough. The earth is producing plenty of food; it is man who is failing in his responsibility to distribute that food properly.

Satan wants to keep you struggling in your finances, in bondage to need and want. He has deceived the people in India into believing it is wrong to eat cows, so every cow in India is left untouched, eating food that should be used to feed the starving nation. If the food reserved for the millions of "sacred" cows was instead used to feed their people, India could practically eliminate their famine crises.

God created more than enough!

I honestly believe the devil has convinced most Christians that they live in a world of scarce resources and tells them they should feel fortunate to live in America – where we have more than most.

We do have more than most, but let me tell you today that there is more than enough for all – in every nation of the world!

But the devil wants to keep you in a poverty mentality. Why? Because he knows the church of God cannot continue to grow through television, through global satellite networks, through multi-language literature, through millions upon millions of debt-free churches without a breed of saints who believe God to give them more than enough!

So the devil has stolen the plank of financial freedom from the holy bridge.

Let me ask you this question: If Christians do not finance the end-time evangelistic outreach, who will?

The pornographers make millions of dollars in profits by selling smut to America, but no pornographer will ever give one penny to finance the gospel.

No smut movie producer will ever give one dime to finance the next major evangelistic crusade in Europe.

The gospel takes money, but the wealth of the wicked will never finance one penny of any outreach. All television ministries and evangelistic campaigns and churches need money to build the buildings, provide the heat, and to teach the principles of the kingdom of God to every creature...and God is raising up a crop of end-time bankers to make every one of these outreaches possible.

It is time to nail back the plank of financial freedom onto our bridge of God's end-time prosperity.

If you do not need anything – if all your family members are saved; if everyone in your house is so full of the Holy Ghost that people get slain in the Spirit when they walk through your front door; if you have more money than you can spend; if your body is not in any form of pain, infirmity, malady or malfunction; if you have no trouble with your teenagers – then just go on to the next plank in this book.

This chapter is not for anyone like that; anyone like that would not be on this planet!

This chapter is for all of you who are currently trapped in a sense of spiritual poverty – a poverty that affects your health and your wealth!

Our God is a way-maker, a blind-man healer, a leper-cleanser, an abundant provider. He is a healing, delivering, providing, miracle-working Jesus.

Yet, Satan would have you believe there is no financial freedom in the gospel.

Look how backward the world has become in the area of finances.

When you borrow from your own account on plastic and pay eighteen percent or more a year on the money, the world has convinced you that you have "credit."

Wake up. You have a "debit" – you owe the money, and you borrowed it at higher rates than we have seen in our modern-day history.

But you would not be as quick to use your charge card if it was called a DEBIT card. That is too negative a connotation, so the devil has lured the Body of Christ to think in positive terms when they use their "credit" cards.

As a result of easy credit, Christians are in deep debt at an astounding rate; and the devil rejoices. For how can you finance the gospel when you are busy financing the banks of America?

You do not need credit cards; you need the Son of the living God. You need to know how to get in touch with Him, and how to get Him to move on your behalf in every area of your life -- including your finances!

Are you tired of playing church?

Are you tired of going to church and going home, praying to a God you really do not know, never seeing Him move, and never seeing the manifestation of His glory in your finances?

Are you tired of never feeling the overwhelming power of His presence come upon you like a garment?

Are you tired of praying for your finances month after month and still finding yourself deeper and deeper in debt?

Well, I have news for you. *If you need something today that you did not have yesterday, then you have to do something different today than the way you were doing it yesterday.*

It is time to throw away the traditional religious ideas of how we pray, of how God wants us to flounder in a poverty mentality; the traditional religious ideas are not getting it done!

The church is still sick, still broke; and the world is still going to hell.

It is time to change something.

Who Sealed Up Those Heavenly Windows?

Malachi 3:10 says, **"...prove me now...if I will not open you the windows of heaven, and pour you out a blessing, that there shall not be room enough to receive it."**

I do not care whether the world likes that or not. I serve a God who promises He will supply all my needs. I am tired of letting this world dictate to me what the Bible supposedly says!

Satan has bound the Body of Christ, and he has lied. We have conjured up a puny little vision of who we think God is. It is not for us to decide who God is; He has already declared who He is.

The Body of Christ believed in biblical prosperity until the secular press lambasted the concepts. We sinned by accepting the devil's lies and making Christians ashamed of the blessings of God on their lives. We have said, "Don't wear that; don't drive that; and don't live there."

It is time we said, "Satan, you didn't give it to me; and you're not going to take it away. It is none of your business how I am blessed. I am the apple of God's eyes. I am the righteousness of God in Christ Jesus. Jesus shed His blood for me, and my God created more than enough for all of us."

Give Up What You Want

To begin to erase your current poverty mentality and to begin to help you understand the biblical principles which will release God's abundant blessings into your life, we can start by looking at the lesson God teaches us in Hannah.

Hannah was the mother of Samuel the prophet, one of the greatest prophets in biblical history. Samuel was the last Judge of Israel, and he anointed both Saul and David to be kings of Israel. It is little wonder then that Satan had a vested interest in keeping Samuel from being born.

Let us look at his story in 1 Samuel chapter 1.

Hannah was barren; she could have no children. She had been believing God for a child, praying, and praying, and praying. She prayed until it felt like her tongue was going to fall out on the floor, but there was no apparent answer. She felt like the heavens were brass.

It seemed to her as though God was only answering other people's prayers, moving for everyone else but her. It seemed like everyone else could feel the touch of God, receive deliverance, experience healing – but not her.

Have you ever felt that way? Have you ever watched your neighbors buy a new car, go on an exotic vacation, or spend thousands of dollars to landscape their yard while you are barely able to keep your bills ahead of the collection phone calls?

If you have experienced those frustrations, then you understand Hannah a bit better. She was a faithful woman, a woman of prayer.

But it is not enough just to pray; you must pray with your God-given authority.

You cannot ask the devil if he would like to leave; tell him!

Pray with authority.

You cannot pray with authority when your heart is full of sin; you cannot pray with authority when you have bitterness in your heart. You must pray in the manner the Bible instructs.

I cannot find any place in the Bible where anyone ever folded their hands to pray or closed their eyes; yet, 99 percent of the church world says, "Let us fold our hands and bow our heads and close our eyes."

Why not lift up our heads, open our eyes, and come out of the closet!

We have enough "Secret Service Christians" – it is time to let the devil know we are in town. "Hey, we're here, Devil! And greater is He that is in us than he that is in the world."

It is not enough just to pray.

Hannah prayed for years.

Everyone in the neighborhood knew her prayer.

Finally, she became weary of not getting her answer; she became discouraged with the heavens being as brass. She began to question, "God, are You who You say You are?"

As she uttered this question, I am sure all the religious people of her day told her to be quiet.

"You shouldn't talk to God that way."

In her heart she said, "Wait a minute, God said He'd answer me. God, are You a liar? Here I am. I've prayed and I've prayed, and no answer, no son. I still have a barren womb. I'm a laughing stock. God, don't You care?"

Her desperation reminds me of the disciples when Jesus said, "Let's go over to the other side of the Sea of Galilee." They jumped in the boat and the lightning started flashing out of a dark-throated storm cloud. The wind was blustering in their faces; the clouds were rolling; and the seas were seething. The little boat was tossed to and fro, and they thought surely they would drown.

Finally, one of the disciples had enough sense to go down in the bottom of the boat and wake Jesus up. Some of you are going to have to go down into the bottom of your boat and wake Jesus up. Wake Him up; stir Him up, down, on the inside; get Him stirred up.

He is brighter than the lightning, louder than the thunder, bigger than your bills. He clapped His hands and the world came into being.

The religious world will tell you, "Now you can't do that. You must be real nice."

It is not time to be nice.

> **"And from the days of John the Baptist until now the kingdom of heaven suffereth violence, and the violent take it by force."**
>
> **Matthew 11:12**

It is time for you to get violent in your spirit, to stand in front of hell; reach one hand up into the glory of God and the other down into the gutter of the life of your family and say, "In the name of Jesus, Devil, my loved ones are not going to hell. In the name of Jesus, I am going to give 30 percent of my income to the church – after all, I have more than enough."

Become violent enough to let the devil know you absolutely mean business. If the Word of God is not true, then we might as well throw our Bibles out the side door into a huge pile, light a fire under them, have a wienie roast, and go home.

Remember Me, God?

We are not serving a halfway God, an almost God, a God that answers prayer sometimes. God said in Jeremiah 33:3, **"Call unto me, and I will answer thee…"**

I will answer thee.

> **"For verily I say unto you, That whosoever shall say unto this mountain, Be thou removed, and be thou cast into the sea; and shall not doubt in his heart, but shall believe that those things which he saith shall come to pass; he shall have whatsoever he saith. Therefore I say unto you, What things soever ye desire, when**

ye pray, believe that ye receive them, and ye shall have
them."

Mark 11:23-24

"...Ask, and it shall be given you; seek, and ye
shall find; knock, and it shall be opened unto you."

Luke 11:9

"...Whatsoever ye shall ask the Father in my name,
he will give it you. Hitherto have ye asked nothing in
my name: ask, and ye shall receive..."

John 16:23-24

The devil has duped you long enough.

You do not have to be satisfied with unanswered prayers.

You just need to learn how to pray with authority.

A dear friend of mine was deeply involved in "prayer" one
evening. He said it was as if God tapped him on the shoulder and
asked him, "What are you doing?"

His answer was, "I'm praying."

God said, "No, you're not; you're complaining."

Hannah said, "I've had enough of this." You have to get to the
point in your life where enough is enough.

The problem with most Christians is that the devil allows
enough blessings into their lives to keep them satisfied and paci-
fied.

Some of you have been sucking on a pacifier when God has
milk to feed you. You have been satisfied with the pacification of
the devil, but your belly is still hungry. It is time to take that pacifier out of your mouth and say, "God, I'm looking for the real
thing."

First Samuel 1:9-10 states:

**"So Hannah rose up after they had eaten in Shiloh,
and after they had drunk. Now Eli the priest sat upon a**

seat by a post of the temple of the Lord. And she was in bitterness of soul, and prayed unto the Lord, and wept sore."

Now, the most unorthodox, theologically incorrect prayer in the entire Bible is fond in the next verse, verse 11.

"And she vowed a vow, and said, O Lord of hosts, if thou wilt indeed look on the affliction of thine handmaid, and remember me..."

She said, "If thou wilt remember me."

Most preachers would tell you not ever to pray like that. She had the audacity to think God had forgotten her!

God never forgets you, but He loves to be reminded that you are there. In fact, His Word declares, "Remind Me of the promises that I have made unto you."

Abraham said, "Lord, remember thy servant."

Moses said, "God, don't forget about me."

Hannah declared, "Lord, remember me."

You need to quit being so timid about God. You are not going to scare Him off. He does not have stage fright. He is not timid about leaping onto the stage of your life. He is not shy about who is watching Him.

In fact, God likes a crowd. He told Elijah to call out all the prophets of Baal in 1 Kings 18:19. "You pour water over that sacrifice and the god that answers by fire, He will be God." God said, "Draw me a crowd. I am about to display My splendor."

Some of you have forgotten about the promises God has made to you.

My cry is, "Remember me, Lord, little Rod Parsley here. I just want to remind You that You said I'd be blessed coming in and going out. Don't forget me, Lord. You said You were the Lord God who healed all my diseases. I just want to remind You, Lord, You are my healer. You are my provider."

The religious world seems to think they know how to accomplish the evangelization of the world; yet, they never seem to achieve that goal.

We are no longer interested in rhetoric; we want results. We do not want talk; we want a triumphant testimony of the power of God. We do not want just a sign; we want substance. We do not want just a message; we want a miracle.

I believe God has a clear plan for us to get what we want.

I am tired of the world dictating to the church the nature of our God. The world has no revelation of God, and they have no understanding of the things of God. They think the only way to be healed is to pay a doctor great sums of money.

That is not the only way to get healed. Thank God for doctors, but they are not the only way.

The world thinks the only way to become financially prosperous is to lie, cheat, and steal.

There is another way. It is called **"Give, and it shall be given unto you; good measure, pressed down, and shaken together, and running over" (Luke 6:38).** That is God's way of saying, "Let Me see if there's room for Me to bless you any more."

Breaking With Tradition

I have a preacher friend who needed to pay off his church building; the loan was for about $250,000. He had a struggling church, a great debt, and seemingly, no way out.

One day, a man who normally went to another church came and sat in one of his meetings. After the meeting, the man came up to the pastor and said, "I don't like you. I don't like this church. I don't like the way you preach; I don't like all that sweating and screaming. I just want you to know I don't even like what you preach."

Then the man turned around and left.

A couple of weeks later, the same man showed up at this pastor's office and said, "I want you to know I don't like you. I don't like what you preach, and I don't like the way you preach it; but I can't get away from it. I'm not going to come to your church, but I've come here today because I have some kind of inside compulsion that I cannot get away from. I have come here to write out a check to pay off this building, but I don't even like you.

Now that is the kind of testimony I like!

I am telling you, **"...the wealth of the sinner is laid up for the just" (Proverbs 13:22).** We are going to get it; and, believe me, they do not like it!

Get in your spirit, God wants you to prosper.

"For God giveth to a man that is good in his sight wisdom, and knowledge, and joy: but to the sinner he giveth travail, to gather and to heap up, that he may give to him that is good before God."

Ecclesiastes 2:26

Start to shake off that religious tradition that wants to keep you on your way to hell, that wants to keep your body sick, and now is working overtime to keep you poor. Poverty is a diabolical lie of the darkened, demonic underworld.

God wants you to have wealth.

"But thou shalt remember the Lord thy God: for it is he that giveth thee power to get wealth, that he may establish his covenant which he sware unto thy fathers, as it is this day."

Deuteronomy 8:18

God has given YOU the power to get wealth!
Why?
So you can establish His covenant – so you can bring the gospel to the lost souls around the world.

Do not ever be ashamed of the blessings of God on you. Just throw your head back and say, "Bless me, God. Bless me until I can't stand it."

I am talking about abundance in every area of your life.

Some of you have allowed the devil to steal your prosperity. You once were after it; you once were in pursuit of it; you once were believing God for it. You once were searching the scriptures to find out how to produce prosperity in your life so that the gospel could be preached; but now you have allowed the devil to steal it away.

You may say, "I just don't believe we ought to have such excess wealth in this life." Well, then feel free to give yours away! No one said you had to keep it all.

I am stirred up about this. It is time we broke the curse. It is time we started believing God's Word; it is time we started believing His prophets. As we do, we will prosper.

"...Believe in the Lord your God, so shall ye be established; believe his prophets, so shall ye prosper."

2 Chronicles 20:20

It is time to shut the devil's mouth and be blessed, whether the devil likes it or not.

Break with tradition. Break with the world. Break with the way you have been doing things, if you are going to have something you have never had before.

It is time to get your prayers answered!

In Psalm 19, David cried out to God to forgive him of the great iniquity.

Was the great iniquity adultery?

No.

Was it murder?

No.

David says that the great iniquity is presumption. David was an adulterer and a murderer, but he said the great iniquity was presuming something about God that was not true.

We have presumed a concept of God that is not true. He is not some religious golden calf but a God of awesome power, a God who has made promises to you that He will keep.

Hannah said, "I've been going in a little religious circle, through the religious rudiments, through the motions. I have been going to Sunday morning service, sticking my hands up in the air, doing everything that looks religious; but it is not working."

Part of the problem in this affluent, sin-sick society we are living in is that we are not needy enough. Whenever there is a world crisis or a war going on, we have to set up folding chairs in our church on Sunday morning to accommodate the crowds. But when the urgent need is removed, the people that once flooded our church disappear.

It is time we wake up.

We do not think we are needy any more. Our trembling hands are reaching out for a hand bigger than ours. We are not jumping over the pews and falling over the altars any more.

Why?

Ungodly affluence.

We have the best doctors, the best lawyers, padded pews, crystal chandeliers; we think we have no need of anything else. When we get needy enough, when we get desperate enough, we will do things differently.

Time for a Change

Hannah was at the point where she said, "I'll do anything. I don't care if the religious people like it. I don't care if the news media likes it. I don't give two holy hoots whether the denomination likes it. I'm not asking the third floor of headquarters whether they like it; they're not the ones with the barren womb. They're not the ones whose prayers are going unanswered."

Hannah said of her own religious leaders, "Maybe they've not had enough yet. But as for me, I've had enough. I want my prayers answered. And if it means breaking with tradition, so be it. If it means they don't allow me to be a part of their little social club, so be it. If it means they don't invite me to their ecumenical party, so be it. If it means they don't ask me to preach at their camp meeting, so be it. But as for me, I'm seeking out my own salvation in fear and trembling before God; and I'm going to see my prayers answered."

It is time to change something.

If your family is about to split the bowels of hell wide open, it is enough.

If you are tired of being sick, it is enough.

If your bills are always behind, if your house is in danger of going back to the bank, it is enough.

We must change something.

Hannah said, "This is it. I'm breaking with tradition. I'm breaking with what everybody else things about it. I'm breaking with everybody else's little idea of who they think God is. I'm going to find out who He is.

> **"And she vowed a vow, and said, O Lord of hosts, if thou wilt indeed look on the affliction of thine handmaid, and remember me, and not forget thine handmaid, but wilt give unto thine handmaid a man child, then I will give him unto the Lord all the days of his life, and there shall no razor come upon his head."**
>
> **1 Samuel 1:11**

Now, Hannah's prayer would not be much of a story if it stopped here. So look at the 19th verse.

> **"And they rose up in the morning early, and worshipped before the Lord, and returned, and came to their house to Ramah: and Elkanah knew Hannah his wife; and the Lord remembered her."**

After years of praying, the Lord remembered her, and she bore a son, and then six more besides him. When God opens the floodgates, the floodgates are open! She asked for one son, not seven. She prayed, "God, I vow a vow. If You give me one, I'll give him back to You."

God gave her one, and she gave him back. Then God opened the floodgates of heaven and poured her out a blessing there was not room enough to contain!

Our God is the God of more than enough. When we purpose in our heart to give to God, He will open and pour.

There was a man who had two pigs; and he said, "God, if You'll give me ten, I'll give You five.

God replied, "No, you won't. You have two and you won't give Me one."

But Hannah prayed, "Lord, I have none. You give me one and I'll give him back to You."

Do you see the difference?"

She offered her only son up to God.

She understood the law of sowing and reaping. You must plant what you lack. If you want apples, plant apple seeds. If you lack oranges, plant orange seeds. Hannah lacked children, so she agreed to sow her first child back to God.

She put him in the house of God to be raised up as a priest and a prophet. She let go of him – totally and completely.

And what happened?

God's law says, **"Give, and it shall be given unto you..." (Luke 6:38).**

She let go of one son, and God opened her womb so she started to have one baby a year. Finally, she cried out, "Okay, God, seven is enough. That's the perfect number. What do You say we just cut this thing off about now?"

You say, "Are you telling me Hannah was blessed because she was willing to give everything up?"

Sure. Look at the Israelites and Moses.

Moses came down out of the mountain of God and said, "Tell the people we need to build the temple. Tell them to bring their earrings and their jewelry, to get their money out of stocks and bonds and get it into the work of God. Tell them to get it wherever they can get it and bring it in and make it an offering unto the Lord to build the Lord's house."

Moses declared, "Everyone that is of a willing heart, let him give unto the Lord for the building of this house" (Exodus 25:2).

The people gave freely.

Finally, Moses had to stand on the heaps of gold and silver, on the robes, on the piles of diamonds and rubies, and plead with them, saying "Stop!"

Hannah had to say, "Stop! My God, I've opened up a thing here I can't get closed!"

Building Your Prayer Wall

In Acts 10, we have a tremendous testimony about a man named Cornelius, who mixed his prayer with his giving. This one soldier was responsible for the message of salvation, healing, and deliverance coming to his entire household and to all the non-Jewish people of the world.

Cornelius had been praying. The Bible says Cornelius was **"...a centurion of the band called the Italian band, A devout man, and one that feared God with all his house, which gave much alms to the people, and prayed to God always" (Acts 10:1-2).**

Understand that Cornelius was a tradition-smasher.

Tradition says, "God might heal you," but faith in God's Word says, "Your healing has been bought and paid for."

It is a fact, not a promise.

Cornelius was praying to the God of the Jews, and he was a Gentile; he knew if he was going to get anywhere with God, he was going to have to break with tradition.

If you are ever going to get something you have never had, you are going to have to do something you have never done.

Notice that Cornelius gave alms to the people and prayed to God. That is a powerful combination. Do you know what alms are? A one-word definition for "alms" is "money." He gave money and prayed to God always.

Of course, there is no price you can pay for any part of the salvation package. You can no more buy healing than you can salvation, but the proof of desire is in pursuit. In God's Word, sincerity is proven by sacrifice.

Jesus said, "If you love Me, keep My commandments."

If I were in need of healing or anything else from God, I would want Him to know I mean business. God's Word teaches us that what I make happen for someone else, God will make happen for me (Luke 6:36-38).

About the ninth hour one day, an angel of God appeared to Cornelius. When Cornelius looked on him, he was afraid and said, "What is it, Lord?"

The angel said to him, **"…Thy prayers and thine alms are come up for a memorial before God. And now send men to Joppa, and call for one Simon, whose surname is Peter" (Acts 10:4-5).**

His prayers and his giving had built a prayer wall of remembrance before God!

The Apostle Peter had been praying on a housetop in the town of Joppa. He saw a sheet let down from heaven, and inside that sheet were all manner of unclean beasts. The Lord said, "Get up, Peter, and slay and eat."

Peter said, "I can't do it, Lord. That stuff is unclean."

God said to him, "Peter, don't call unclean what I have called clean."

God answered Cornelius' prayer and prepared Peter in a vision to come and bring salvation and the message of healing and deliverance to the entire Gentile world!

Cornelius had a need: he and his family needed salvation. The spiritual principle he put into motion works for whatever need you have. Cornelius not only prayed, he prayed and gave; and the Bible says that his alms and prayers were come up for a memorial before God.

When giving becomes the mortar and prayer the bricks, you can build a wall of memorial before the face of God. Satan has no trouble breaking down a wall of bricks without mortar, but he will break his foot if he tries to kick over prayers held together with giving.

Hannah went from unanswered prayer to an outright deluge of abundance because she vowed a vow and kept it. Her vow made her remembered in the eyes of God.

Hannah mixed her giving with her praying. She said, "It is not important to me whether I get to keep all of it or not; it is only important to me that I receive it." She said, "God, You give it to me; I'll give it back to You."

The Bible does not say, "My children will run and try to find a little trickle of My blessing."

The Bible says it will find you; it will overtake you; and you won't be able to get away from it. God's Word says, **"Give, and it shall be given unto you; good measure, pressed down, and shaken together, and running over..." (Luke 6:38).**

How to Start the Flow

The majority of the time the problem is not how to get the blessings to stop but rather how, under God, do we get them to start?

You will not start receiving your abundant blessings by doing what the world or the "twice dead and plucked up by the roots," religious church crowd thinks you should do. If you do what they do, all you are going to receive is what they have.

I do not want to look like I slept upside down in a posthole, like I bounced off the back of a covered wagon, like I am eating out of trash cans, like I am living out of a food pantry, or like I am getting my clothes from the missionary barrel.

I have had enough of that.

You can keep it if you want to. I will endure the persecution that comes with the blessing.

Why hasn't the Body of Christ received this truth?

Why are we not living this reality?

I am telling you, if you will pray God's way, God can open up whatever you need opened up in your life. Your prayer, mixed with giving, will become a memorial before God. He will open the windows of heaven for you the same way He opened Hannah's womb; your blessing will start pouring forth until you cannot stop it. What God opens, no man can close.

Endnotes

[1] Roberts Liardon, *Kathryn Kuhlman: A Spiritual Biography of God's Miracle Working Power* (Tulsa: Harrison House, 1990), pp. 130-132.

[2] "Official Gold Reserves." *Wikipedia.* (23 April, 2006) <http://en.wikipedia.org/wiki/Gold_reserves.html> (April 27, 2006).

[3] "World Silver Survey 2005: A Summary." *The Silver Institute.* (July 2005). <http://www.silverinstitute.org/wssum05.pdf> (April 27, 2006).

[4] Hutzler, Mary J., "Statement of Mary J. Hutzler: Energy Information Administration Department of Energy before the Subcommittee on Energy and Air Quality Committee on Energy and Commerce; United States House of Representatives, Hearing on Coal." (March 14, 2001). <http://tonto.eia.doe.gov/FTPROOT/presentations/oiaf/speeches/314eia.html> (April 25, 2006).

[5] Paul, Ron. "New Money, Old Excuses." *The New American, Vol. 10, Number 18.* (September 5, 1994). <http://www.hackcanada.com/blackcrawl/patriot/money_changes.txt> (April 25, 2006).

[6] Aizcorbe, Ana M., Kennickell, Arthur B., and Moore, Kevin B. "Recent Changes in U.S. Family Finances: Evidence from the 1998 and 2001 Survey of Consumer Finances," *Federal Reserve Bulletin,* 89 (January 2003): 1-32. <http://www.federalreserve.gov/pubs/oss/oss2/2001/scf2001home.html> (April 25, 2006).

Your Financial Freedom Tool Kit

Here Are the Tools, the Spiritual Hammer and Nails, You Need to Biblically Repair and Restore the Financial Freedom Plank in Your Life.

I.   Jesus, Who Was Rich, Became Poor That Those Who are Poor Might Become Rich

2 Corinthians 8:7 Therefore, as ye abound in every thing, in faith, and utterance, and knowledge, and in all diligence, and in your love to us, see that ye abound in this grace also.

v. 8 I speak not by commandment, but by occasion of the forwardness of others, and to prove the sincerity of your love.

v. 9 For ye know the grace of our Lord Jesus Christ, that, though he was rich, yet for your sakes he became poor, that ye through his poverty might be rich.

Deuteronomy 8:17 And thou say in thine heart, My power and the might of mine hand hath gotten me this wealth.

v. 18 But thou shalt remember the Lord thy God: for it is he that giveth thee power to get wealth, that he may establish his covenant which he sware unto thy fathers, as it is this day.

Isaiah 48:17 Thus saith the Lord, thy Redeemer, the Holy One of Israel; I am the Lord thy God which teacheth thee to profit, which leadeth thee by the way that thou shouldest go.

2 Chronicles 26:5 And he sought God in the days of Zechariah, who had understanding in the visions of God: and as long as he sought the Lord, God made him to prosper.

Genesis 24:40 And he said unto me, The Lord, before whom I walk, will send his angel with thee, and prosper thy way; and thou shalt take a wife for my son of my kindred, and of my father's house.

II. Riches Must Not Be Our Priority

Matthew 6:33 But seek ye first the kingdom of God, and his righteousness; and all these things shall be added unto you.

2 Peter 1:3 According as his divine power hath given unto us all things that pertain unto life and godliness, through the knowledge of him that hath called us to glory and virtue.

III. The Key is Obedience

Isaiah 1:19 If ye be willing and obedient, ye shall eat the good of the land.

Job 36:11 If they obey and serve him, they shall spend their days in prosperity, and their years in pleasures.

Luke 6:38 Give, and it shall be given unto you; good measure, pressed down, and shaken together, and running over, shall men give into your bosom. For with the same measure that ye mete withal it shall be measured to you again.

Deuteronomy 28:11 And the Lord shall make thee plenteous in goods, in the fruit of thy body, and in the fruit of thy cattle, and in the fruit of thy ground, in the land which the Lord sware unto thy fathers to give thee.

Genesis 26:12 Then Isaac sowed in that land, and received in the same year an hundredfold: and the Lord blessed him.

v. 13 And the man waxed great, and went forward, and grew until he became very great.

Romans 8:31 What shall we then say to these things? If God be for us, who can be against us?

v. 32 He that spared not his own Son, but delivered him up for us all, how shall he not with him also freely give us all things?

IV. The Purpose of Divine Prosperity Is To Build the Kingdom

Nehemiah 2:20 Then answered I them, and said unto them, The God of heaven, he will prosper us; therefore we his servants will arise and build: but ye have no portion, nor right, nor memorial, in Jerusalem.

Proverbs 10:22 The blessing of the Lord, it maketh rich, and he addeth no sorrow with it.

Proverbs 13:22 A good man leaveth an inheritance to his children's children: and the wealth of the sinner is laid up for the just.

Proverbs 23:3 Be not desirous of his dainties: for they are deceitful meat.

v. 4 Labour not to be rich: cease from thine own wisdom.

Proverbs 22:9 He that hath a bountiful eye shall be blessed; for he giveth of his bread to the poor.

V. The Good News (Gospel) to the Poor Is That You Do Not Have to be Poor Anymore

Luke 4:18 The Spirit of the Lord is upon me, because he hath anointed me to preach the gospel to the poor; he hath sent me to heal the brokenhearted, to preach deliverance to the captives, and recovering of sight to the blind, to set at liberty them that are bruised,

v. 19 To preach the acceptable year of the Lord.

Psalm 68:19 Blessed be the Lord, who daily loadeth us with benefits, even the God of our salvation. Selah.

Psalm 112:1 Praise ye the Lord. Blessed is the man that feareth the Lord, that delighteth greatly in his commandments.

Psalm 112:3 Wealth and riches shall be in his house: and his righteousness endureth for ever.

Psalm 50:10 For every beast of the forest is mine, and the cattle upon a thousand hills.

Psalm 50:12 If I were hungry, I would not tell thee: for the world is mine, and the fulness thereof.

Haggai 2:8 The silver is mine, and the gold is mine, saith the Lord of hosts.

1 Corinthians 10:26 For the earth is the Lord's and the fullness thereof.

Proverbs 8:21 That I may cause those that love me to inherit substance; and I will fill their treasures.

3 John 2 Beloved, I wish above all things that thou mayest prosper and be in health, even as thy soul prospereth.

PLANK SEVEN

Restoring Hope to the
Body of Christ

PLANK SEVEN

Restoring Hope to the Body of Christ

Come Forth

Before the tomb Christ stood one day,
And dried the people's tears away
As He spoke forth in mighty voice
That made Judea's hills rejoice,
              "Come forth!"

Inside the tomb Christ lay one morn,
Defeated seemed Salvation's Horn,
But God the Father spoke the word,
And this He said, though no man heard,
              "Come forth!"

Inside the tomb of sin I lay,
The price of sin I had to pay;
But Christ the Raiser of the dead
Spoke to my poor, bound soul and said,
              "Come forth!"

And when the great and final sound
Shall raise our loved ones from the ground,
'Twill be the last time we shall hear
That glorious sound upon our ear,
              "Come forth!"

— Louie W. Stokes[1]

One Minute to Midnight!

Satan wants you discouraged – he wants you to despair at the events unfolding in your world, to give up all hope of any meaningful future for you or your children. To rob you of your hope, he constantly reminds you of the pathetic condition of your present world.

The devil wants your eyes to focus on the AIDS epidemic running rampant. He wants you to see and participate in the perverse sexual sins ripping apart our families and Christian marriages.

The devil wants to rob you of any hope for the future by focusing your eyes on the high rate of divorce in the Christian world and by telling you, "It will only get worse. You can't even trust your spiritual leaders. Look at the religious sex and financial scandals rocking American Christianity. You might as well give up all hope."

I have news for the devil – he is doomed; he is the only one who is living without hope.

You and I are living in the end-time generation of spiritual history, and we have the *blessed hope* of the second coming of Jesus Christ when He will rule and reign!

Know the Hour

Listen.

Listen carefully.

Can you hear it?

Listen to the ticking of the second hand on God's end-time clock.

With each passing second, you and I are ever closer to the final moments of end-time spiritual history.

It is one minute to midnight, and I fully believe we are in the final countdown.

God's holy Word declares there shall be signs happening around the world to signal the second coming of our Savior, Jesus Christ!

The clock is ticking.

In this final minute of spiritual history, God wants you to know His end-time plan – so you can rest in His Word and so you can place your trust and your hope in Him!

Recognize the End-time Signs

There are several major events happening in the world today that you need to see through spiritual eyes so you can recognize that we are living in the final minute of spiritual history.

God wants you to know His plan!

As you recognize His hand in the major events unfolding in the world today, your faith will increase; and the Holy Ghost will begin to restore the plank of HOPE Satan has stolen from your life.

Here are five of the major end-time signs unfolding right now that clearly demonstrate God is in control of this world and that His end-time plan for your life is unfolding – NOW!

1. Conflicts in Our World – With No Way Out!

"And there shall be signs in the sun, and in the moon, and in the stars; and upon the earth distress of nations, with perplexity; the sea and the waves roaring."

Luke 21:25

War has always been a part of man's history; but never before has there been so many continuing conflicts in the world, such "distress of nations" – with no clear solutions, with no way out!

The United Nations defines "major wars" as military conflicts inflicting 1,000 battlefield deaths per year. In 1965, there were 10 major wars under way. The new millennium began with much of the world consumed in armed conflict or cultivating an uncertain peace. As of mid-2005, there were eight major wars under way [down from 15 at the end of 2003], with as many as two dozen "lesser" conflicts ongoing with varying degrees of intensity.

Most victims of these current civil wars are civilians, a feature that distinguishes modern conflicts. During World War I, civilians made up fewer than 5 percent of all casualties. Today, 75 percent or more of those killed or wounded in wars are non-combatants.

Africa, to a greater extent than any other continent, is afflicted by war. Africa has been marred by more than 20 major civil wars since 1960. Rwanda, Somalia, Angola, Sudan, Liberia, and Burundi are among those countries that have recently suffered serious armed conflict. [2]

In Israel, war has become a way of life. Terrorist groups employ unconventional military tactics to undermine Israel's peace. Hijackings, car bombings, and even kamikaze-type attacks are employed to disrupt Israel's day-to-day living. There seems to be no earthly solutions to the Palestinian/Israeli conflict that consistently undermines the security of Israel.

2. Famine, Pestilence and Earthquakes in Our Land

"And great EARTHQUAKES shall be in divers places, and FAMINES, and PESTILENCES; and fearful sights and great signs shall there be from heaven."

Luke 21:11

The presence of worldwide famines at a time in our history when there should be no *famines* – makes this time unique. The major wheat producers of the world grow enough wheat to feed every starving person in the world; yet, to keep prices at a "profitable level," much of the wheat is stored or dumped.

As a result of this and other measures, famines abound throughout the world. Millions of Indians are in a massive exodus from the famine area in central India. The northeast section of Brazil has an estimated one million children permanently brain-damaged due to malnutrition resulting from famine. Africa is still experiencing the worst famine in their history with the number of displaced persons in Sudan estimated between 5.3 and 6.2 million during 2005.[3]

Earthquakes have claimed more lives worldwide in the last 5 years than in all of the last 20 years put together—more than 2 times as many lives from 2000 – 2005 than from 1980 – 1999![4]

Pestilence – mystery illnesses such as AIDS – have existed only in this generation. AIDS has already killed more young American men than all those who died in all the battles of the Vietnam War!

3. Miracle Rebirth of Israel

"For I will take you from among the heathen, and gather you out of all countries, and will bring you into your own land."

Ezekiel 36:24

Six million Jews burned in human incinerators during World War II; American bulldozers unearthed untold millions of bones, dry and withered, from the heat of Nazi ovens.[5] Yet, on May 15, 1948, Israel became a nation…overnight! The event marked one of the greatest miracles in history and the fulfillment of an end-time prophecy!

"Who hath heard such a thing? who hath seen such things? Shall the earth be made to bring forth in one day? or shall a nation be born at once? for as soon as Zion travailed, she brought forth her children."

Isaiah 66:8

4. Exploding Increases in Hi-Tech Knowledge

In the past sixty years, there have been more inventions, more discoveries, more scientific and medical breakthroughs than in the entire history of the world! In just the last ten years, man's total knowledge has doubled! It is this astounding magnitude and explosiveness of breakthroughs that sets our generation apart as the end-time generation.

> **"...many shall run to and fro, and knowledge shall be increased."**
>
> **Daniel 12:4**

5. An Escalating End-Time Population

More people than have ever lived in our history – live today. We are seeing end-time prophecy come alive – in the form of "many peoples and nations" living on the earth.

> **"And he said unto me, Thou must prophesy again before many peoples, and nations, and tongues, and kings."**
>
> **Revelation 10:11**

Conservative calculations project that by the year 2050, there will be 10 billion people on the earth!

With each tick of the end-time clock, literally millions of new souls are born into the world. Satan wants to rob every one of them of their hope.

But the devil is a liar!

There is hope, and God has it!

As you see and know His end-time plan for the world and for your life, allow the Holy Ghost to restore the plank of HOPE that the devil has stolen.

He Is Your Hope!

Those who have read the book of Revelation and studied its pages, those who have watered its pages with their tears, are resounding in their cry around the globe today – "Jesus is coming soon!"

There is an old Southern gospel hymn that says, "Loved ones, please listen; I think you should know. If we meet now again in this world below, if death finds me missing and you do not understand, there's an old Book by my bedside that tells where I am" (author unknown).

The Bible has stood the test of time because it is accurate in its predictions. It is the oak of God planted in the forest of eternity, entwining its roots around the rock of ages; and far better men and women than you and I have pillowed their head on it in their dying hour.

Your Bible may say, "The Revelation of St. John the Divine." That is wrong.

It is not a revelation of John.

Revelation 1:1 tells you that it is, **"The Revelation of Jesus Christ, which God gave unto him, to shew unto his servants things which must shortly come to pass…"**

Notice He did not say that they might come to pass or that they would come to pass if everything turned out right. God is not a God of happenstance or circumstance.

He is the God who stood on nothing because there was nothing to stand on, who flung the worlds into their starry existence, who **"measured the waters in the hollow of his hand, and meted out heaven with the span…" (Isaiah 40:12)**. In His majesty he declared, **"I am the first, and I am the last; and beside me there is no God" (Isaiah 44:6)**.

You Are the Proof

You may hear people say, "I do not believe God exists."

Well, tell them to think about this: If you have a watch on your arm, it is proof that somewhere there is a watchmaker. The very fact that you are living, breathing, moving, and in existence is proof positive that somewhere there is a "people-maker."

> **"In the beginning God created the heaven and the earth. And the Lord God planted a garden eastward in Eden; and there he put the man whom he had formed."**
>
> **Genesis 1:1, 2:8**

251

Job said,

**"The spirit of God hath made me, and the breath
of the Almighty hath given me life."**

Job 33:4

If you are alive today, you alone are proof that somewhere you
have a creator. The last book of the Bible talks about Him. It is a
revelation of Jesus Christ. When you see Him in this last book, you
get a different perspective of Him.

Who Is Jesus?

Many perceive Jesus as a spineless, weak-kneed, jellyfish of a
man walking the shore of the blue Galilee Sea, with sandals on His
feet and a flowing, white robe; others add to this picture a man
with long, girlish-looking hair; a thinly-cropped beard, eyes sunk
back in His head (so He looks like He has not had any sleep for the
last 20 years), and show Him cradling a little lamb in His arms.

If that is your image of Jesus, I have news for you – we are not
serving Mary's baby boy born in a manger and wrapped in swad-
dling clothes; we are not serving Joseph's son, the carpenter of
Nazareth; we are not serving Matthew's Messiah or Mark's won-
der-worker, or Luke's Son of God, or John's Son of Man: *We are
serving the resurrected King of kings and Lord of lords, with the keys of
death and hell in His hand!*

**"And I saw heaven opened, and behold a white
horse; and he that sat upon him was called Faithful
and True, and in righteousness he doth judge and
make war."**

Revelation 19:11

Are you getting a little different picture of Him now? Do you
see His long, lean Galilean leg slipping over the back of a steaming

252

white stallion, the crack of His whip billowing out like the crash of a thousand cannons?

Resurrected from the dead, Jesus kicked the end out of the borrowed tomb of Joseph of Arimathaea. He has the nail prints in His flesh to prove that He conquered death and hell by His sinless life, victorious blood, and resurrection from the dead. Now, we see Him riding a glorious white charger.

> **"His eyes were as a flame of fire, and on his head were many drowns..."**
> **Revelation 19:12**

Why is He wearing many crowns?

Because when we walk through that gate hewn of pearl into that great city called the New Jerusalem, we are going to have crowns placed upon our heads, according to our faithfulness in this life. When they are placed on our heads, we are going to run down that heavenly boulevard to the Tree of Life, which bears twelve manner of fruits, the leaves of which are for the healing of the nations (Revelation 22:2).

Jesus has so many crowns on His head because when we get there we are going to throw our crowns at His feet.

Divine Investment

Why do I get happy when I think about heaven?

I have a lot invested there.

When I stroll down the streets of that heavenly city, I will no doubt be stopped by my 19-year-old uncle Danny, who I watched leave for Vietnam, weeping like a little baby, because he did not want to go.

They shipped him home in a body bag.

But I have hope today. He confessed Christ as his Savior, and he was in church every night of his life that it was possible for him to go. Danny will be there on that heavenly boulevard; and no doubt, he will probably tug on my shirt-sleeve. He will probably say, "Come and let me show you David's tabernacle; come and let me show you gates of pearl, that are 300 feet high in a city that is 1,500 miles square."

But I will say, "Danny, it's been a long time since I have seen you, and my heart has longed for the day when we could talk; but, right now, you will have to excuse me. I have an appointment at the throne of God. I have an appointment to bow my knee and worship the Lamb of God who takes away the sin of the world."

Revelation 19:12-16 continues,

> **"His eyes were as a flame of fire, and on his head were many crowns; and he had a name written, that no man knew, but he himself. And he was clothed with a vesture dipped in blood: and his name is called The Word of God. And the armies which were in heaven followed him upon white horses, clothed in fine linen, white and clean. And out of his mouth goeth a sharp sword, that with it he should smite the nations: and he shall rule them with a rod of iron: and he treadeth the winepress of the fierceness and wrath of Almighty God.**

> **"And he hath on his vesture and on his thigh a name written, KING OF KINGS, AND LORD OF LORDS."**

This is the Jesus we are serving today!

> **"And I saw an angel come down from heaven, having the key of the bottomless pit and a great chain in his hand. And he laid hold on the dragon, that old serpent, which is the Devil, and Satan, and bound him a thousand years,**

> **"And cast him into the bottomless pit, and shut him up, and set a seal upon him, that he should de-**

ceive the nations no more, till the thousand years should be fulfilled: and after that he must be loosed a little season.

"And I saw thrones, and they sat upon them, and judgment was given unto them: and I saw the souls of them that were beheaded for the witness of Jesus, and for the word of God, and which had not worshipped the beast, neither his image, neither had received his mark upon their foreheads, or in their hands; and they lived and reigned with Christ a thousand years.

"But the rest of the dead lived not again until the thousand years were finished. This is the first resurrection."

Revelation 20:1-5

Death to Resurrection

If there is a first resurrection, surely there must be a second. I want to share with you the two resurrections.

The first resurrection is the resurrection of the godly to eternal life, in the place that is called heaven. The apostle Paul compares the resurrection of the dead to a grain of wheat sown into the ground (1 Corinthians 15:35-37).

In his gospel, John also likens the resurrection of the dead to a grain of wheat:

"...Except a corn of wheat fall into the ground and die, it abideth alone: but if it die, it bringeth forth much fruit."

John 12:24

There is going to be more than just the resurrection of Jesus of Nazareth. The Bible plainly declares that, "...this corruptible shall

have put on incorruption, and this mortal shall have put on immortality…" (1 Corinthians 15:54).

Let us look back just for a moment and hear the cries of the
mob, "Give us Barabbas; give us Barabbas!"

Pilate asked the crowd, "What shall I do with this man called
Jesus?"

And the crowd called out, "Crucify Him, crucify Him!"

So Pilate threw Jesus to the hands of the angry mob. The
crowd kicked and prodded Jesus through the cobblestone streets of
Jerusalem until He stumbled and fell under the weight of the cross
on which He would pay the sacrificial price for your sins and for
mine.

Simon carried a tremendous burden that day when he lifted the
cross to his own shoulders and helped Jesus toward Calvary. Had
you or I been there, we would probably have drawn back and said,
"That's enough; He's suffered enough."

But no – they spat upon His blood-soaked face, took a crown
of thorns and shoved it into His brow; and, like a lamb being led to
the slaughter, He did not complain.

Jesus had told His disciples, **"…I lay down my life…no man taketh it from me…and I have power to take it again…" (John 10:17-
18)**

They laid His bloody body on that cross, then drove the nails
deep into His flesh; blood spurted from His wounds. All the while,
Jesus was thinking, "I'm doing this for you; I'm doing this for
you."

We want to call to God and say, "Enough! He has suffered
enough! He has bled enough! He has paid enough."

But the Prophet Isaiah said, **"…the Lord hath laid on him the
iniquity of us all" (Isaiah 53:6).** His flesh tore as they swung the
cross up and it fell with a thud into a hole dug in the earth.

"I thirst," He said; and they gave Him vinegar to drink (John
19:28-29).

There He hung, suspended between earth and heaven. He opened His mouth and said, **"Father, forgive them; for they know not what they do" (Luke 23:34).**

The thief on the cross looked over at Him and said, "Master, remember me when You get to Your kingdom. I deserve this, but You have done nothing."

Jesus looked back at him through His bloodstained vision and said, **"...Today shalt thou be with me in paradise" (Luke 23:43).**

His body convulsed; the earth quaked, the lightning crashed out of a dark-throated storm cloud. The afternoon light gave way to darkness as God turned His face from His Son.

Jesus said, **"It is finished: and he bowed his head, and gave up the ghost" (John 19:30).**

But it was not possible that death should hold Him!

David, foreseeing Jesus' day, prophesied, **"For thou wilt not leave my soul in hell; neither wilt thou suffer thine Holy One to see corruption" (Psalm 16:10).**

While sitting upon his imperial throne, Satan thought, "Lazarus was in the tomb four days, and he came out; and Jesus says He is coming out in three. How are we going to keep Him in the grave?" Satan – you cannot do it! There is nothing you can do to stop the Word of God! To stop the blood of Jesus. To stop the love of God. You have tried to crucify it; you have tried to bury it; you have tried to destroy it – but every time you put it in the tomb, it resurrects itself and beats the pallbearers back to the house.

You cannot stop God!

Suddenly a light appeared at the end of the darkness. Jesus lifted the gates of damnation off their rusty hinges, walked up to the throne of the devil, tapped him on the shoulder and said, "Hey, I have a message for you. **'I am he that liveth, and was dead; and, behold, I am alive for evermore, Amen; and have the keys of hell and of death'" (Revelation 1:18).**

He Isn't Here!

Mary came rushing to the tomb on that third morning and found an angel sitting by the empty tomb.

He asked her, "Why do you seek the living among the dead?" That is a question for most of our churches. "Why do you seek the living among the dead?"

It is time for you to get out of that old mausoleum and find a place where they are preaching the fullness and the power of the Word of God! Get into a place where the glory of God is flowing and Jesus is alive! Find a place where signs and wonders are the "amen" of God to the Word that is preached.

Jesus was not the only one resurrected on that first resurrection day.

Graves all over Jerusalem burst open.

Why?

Because **"…now is Christ risen from the dead, and become the firstfruits of them that slept" (1 Corinthians 15:20).**

Jesus brought a sheaf of firstfruits with Him to heaven, not just one staff. Jesus went into the holy of holies and sprinkled His blood on the mercy seat; and the Father said, "Well done."

On Calvary, Jesus said, "It is finished."

At the empty tomb, the Father said, "It is finished." He raised His Son from the dead and painted a six-lane highway of His blood straight through to the New Jerusalem! He declared, "I'm the Alpha and Omega. Come and follow Me. I was dead, but now I'm alive. Because I live, though you were dead, yet shall you live because you believe in Me.

That is resurrection power!

The Bible speaks of yet another phase of the first resurrection.

> **"But I would not have you to be ignorant, brethren, concerning them which are asleep…"**
> **1 Thessalonians 4:13**

Do you realize that a seed of grain, unless it is planted in the ground and dies, remains the same forever? I have heard it said that researchers took some seeds of corn that had been buried in the crypt of King Tutankhamen for thousands of years and planted them in the ground. Those wrinkled up seeds sprang forth to life; first the blade, then the ear, and then the full corn in the ear.

That is resurrection power.

Second Corinthians 5:17 says, **"Therefore if any man be in Christ, he is a new creature: old things are passed away; behold, all things are become new."**

This scripture is not referring to a new address or a new hair color – it is God changing you from the inside out into a new creature who has never existed before.

Unless you die to this world, you will remain the same.

It does not matter how many church services you go to, how many church rolls have your name; it does not matter if you shine the preacher's shoes three times a week or wash the Pope's car – until you die, you will remain the same.

Good works will not get you into heaven, change your life, give you peace when you need it in the midst of the storm, or give you a reason for living when dying looks easy.

Your life will remain the same until you die.

The second death has no power over those who have a part in the first resurrection.

When I was eight years old, I knelt at an old two-by-six altar in a little building that wouldn't seat fifty people, as a woman pastor preached hell so hot I could feel the flames. That day the seed of Rod Parsley was planted and died. I resurrected from the dead that day.

I have fulfilled my quota on dying. You could take out a gun and shoot me and my body would fall over with a thud, but I would not die. My Bible says that when I am absent from the body, I am present with the Lord (2 Corinthians 5:8).

That is resurrection power!

Let us look again at that first resurrection.

259

"I would not have you to be ignorant, brethren, concerning them which are asleep, that ye sorrow not, even as others which have no hope.

"For if we believe that Jesus died and rose again, even so them also which sleep in Jesus will God bring with him.

"For this we say unto you by the word of the Lord, that we which are alive and remain unto the coming of the Lord shall not prevent them which are asleep.

"For the Lord himself shall descend from heaven with a shout, with the voice of the archangel, and with the trump of God: and the dead in Christ shall rise first [that 'great getting-up morning']:

"Then we which are alive and remain shall be caught up together with them in the clouds, to meet the Lord in the air: and so shall we ever be with the Lord."

1 Thessalonians 4:13-17

We are going to be catapulted in an extra-terrestrial fashion into heaven!

"Two women shall be grinding at the mill; the one shall be taken, and the other left."

Matthew 24:41

"...there shall be two...in one bed; the one shall be taken, and the other one shall be left."

Luke 17:34

These scriptures refer to the rapture of the church, the greatest cataclysmic event yet to transpire! I believe it is coming in our generation. I believe that scripture is being fulfilled as fast as the unlocked wheels of time can turn. Jesus is coming like lightning, faster than the fleetest hoof that ever struck the pavement.

"The day of the Lord will come as a thief in the night…" (2 Peter 3:10). He is going to take His church out of this wretched earth, and the dead in Christ are going to resurrect.

What will follow the rapture are seven years which are commonly known as "the tribulation" – seven years of God's determined dealings with the nation of Israel. It is during this time that the Antichrist will reveal himself.

Stop looking for the Antichrist or his number, 666. The church of Jesus Christ will not be here when the Antichrist is unveiled.

Some people say Christians are like coffee pots; coffee pots want to percolate, and Christians want to tribulate. But my Bible says, **"Likewise also as it was in the days of Lot…Even thus shall it be in the day when the Son of man is revealed" (Luke 17:28,30).** Before the first hailstones of fire and brimstone fell out of God's heaven on that immoral city of Sodom, Lot and his family were safely outside.

Three and one-half years into the tribulation period, there is another resurrection. The 144,000 Jewish evangelists who have preached the gospel to the people on earth will be resurrected and raptured, and all of the tribulation saints who have refused to take the mark of the beast will be resurrected and raptured.

Then there is one more resurrection; it appears on the last day of that seven-year period.

The Reign of Christ

The two witnesses appear on the streets of Jerusalem. They have preached the gospel of Christ with signs and wonders, but the Antichrist is given power to slay them. They remain dead in the streets of Jerusalem for three and one-half days; and the Bible says the world will make merry, and men will send gifts one to the other (Revelation 11).

As the world makes merry, the bodies of these two witnesses are left lying in the streets of Jerusalem – their flesh rotting upon their bones. Suddenly, as the television cameras pan the scene for the world to see and rejoice over, the breath of God breathes down; and their decaying eyes pop open.

Suddenly, the two witnesses leap to their feet, and the heavens split open. Jesus stretches out His arms, and those two witnesses are resurrected from the dead and enter the portals of glory.

The last day of the tribulation period signifies the first day of the millennial reign of Christ.

According to Revelation 20:1-3, this millennial reign is the time when the Antichrist and the false prophet are locked up. The angel of God has **"come down from heaven, having the key of the bottomless pit and a great chain in his hand.**

> **"And he laid hold on the dragon, that old serpent, which is the Devil, and Satan, and bound him a thousand years.**

> **"And cast him into the bottomless pit, and shut him up, and set a seal upon him, that he should deceive the nations no more, till the thousand years be fulfilled: and after that he must be loosed a little season."**

Revelation 20:5-8 tells us:

> **"...the rest of the dead lived not again until the thousand years were finished. This is [the end of] the first resurrection.**

> **"Blessed and holy is he that hath part in the first resurrection: on such the second death hath no power, but they shall be priests of God and of Christ, and shall reign with him a thousand years.**

"And when the thousand years are expired, Satan shall be loosed out of his prison, And shall go out to deceive the nations..."

During that thousand years, Christians will rule and reign with Christ on the face of the earth. People will live and breathe, reproduce and multiply during that thousand years. They will serve Jesus because the devil will be bound.

There will be no sickness, no disease. The Bible says that during this thousand years, the lion will lay down with the lamb; and in that day, if a young child should put his hand in the hold of an asp, he should have no hurt (Isaiah 11:6-9).

We are going to rule and reign over the nations of the earth for a thousand years; and at the end of that thousand years, the devil must be loosed out of his prison for a little while.

Why must he be loosed?

Nations have been born, and they have served God because the devil was bound; they have had no opportunity to choose between God and the devil. Satan will be let out for a little while, and he will go forth on the face of the earth to deceive the nations.

Many will follow the devil; many will follow Jesus.

At the end of that period, Revelation 20:8 says they will gather themselves together to battle from the four quarters of the earth to oppose God from Gog and Magog (do not mistake this for the battle of Armageddon which transpires on the last day of the tribulation period). This is the last day of the millennial reign, and this multitude will come against the camp of the saints. The next verse (Revelation 20:9) declares, **"... and fire came down from God out of heaven, and devoured them."**

On the last day of the millennial reign of Christ, the righteous from Adam until that moment – the redeemed, ransomed, and washed in the blood of the Lamb – will stand with God on the side of His throne when the second resurrection transpires.

"And I saw a great white throne, and him that sat on it, from whose face the earth and the heaven fled away; and there was found no place for them.

"And I saw the dead, small and great, stand before God; and the books were opened: and another book was opened, which is the book of life: and the dead were judged out of those things which were written in the books, according to their works.

"And the sea gave up the dead which were in it; and death and hell delivered up the dead which were in them: and they were judged every man according to their works.

"And death and hell were cast into the lake of fire. This is the second death. And whosoever was not found written in the book of life was cast into the lake of fire.

Revelation 20:11-15

This is the resurrection of the wicked dead from the time of Adam until the last day of the millennial reign of Christ.

The Final Judgment

All adulterers will be there, all whoremongers, and all liars. The offscouring of the earth will be there. The moon will be bleeding and the seas will be seething under the whiplash of fury as they spill their dead into the lap of God. Some will have been in hell for thousands of years, when suddenly hell's gates will be opened; and they will be called out.

Can you imagine what will happen when they think they have received a reprieve and the place of damnation belches them out before the throne of God?

Suddenly, they are free from the torment of the fire that burns day and night. Suddenly, the gates are opened, and they find themselves before the throne of God.

They will think, "Surely something has happened; surely God Himself has sent down a reprieve. Surely we have suffered long enough. Surely we have chewed our tongues for pain long enough. Surely now God is letting us out of the burning inferno of hell."

They see those gates that are 300 feet high carved out of a single pearl; they see the new Jerusalem; they see a land where there are no wheelchairs, no hospitals, no crutches, no ambulances – for the former things have passed away.

They see the throne of God. They see the sainted millions. They see the angels with folded wings, standing at attention. They see the Lamb of God sitting upon His throne, and they are just waiting for Him to unlock the gates of that city and let them in.

Then suddenly, the gavel of God's justice comes down with a thundering clap. He says, "You have been brought here to be judged."

Oh, the horror that will grip their minds!

They see the celestial city, but their feet will never touch those streets of gold. They will never hear the words they long to hear drop from the lips of God: **"Well done, thou good and faithful servant...enter thou into the joy of thy lord" (Matthew 25:21).**

They are told they can never come in. Daddies will see their babies; husbands will see their wives. They will say, "Why didn't I listen? God, please give me just one more chance."

But in that day there will be no stay of execution. There will be no reprieve from the governor's office. God will say, "Depart from Me, ye workers of iniquity; I never knew you. Enter into the lake of fire where the smoke belches up with your pain for all of eternity. Depart from Me; I never knew you" (Matthew 25:41).

They will wail and scream.

Have you ever been in a courtroom and heard the sound when the judge's gavel comes down and the verdict was, "Guilty as charged"? Have you seen men sentenced to die in the electric chair? Have you heard their friends and relatives cry out? These tragedies will not compare to God's day of judgment, and will pale in significance to the procession of the dead on that great day.

Who will be there?

The murderers and the whoremongers will be there. But so will millions of good people – millions who counted on their rosaries, who looked to Buddha, who followed philosophy, who trusted in the New Age movement.

There will be millions who paid their taxes, who never stole anything from anyone. There will be millions who waited one day too late, who resisted one altar call too many; millions who said there is some other way to heaven except by the blood of the Lamb.

And on that day they, too, will be separated forever.

The rich young ruler will be there. He will say, "Jesus, I'll give up all that I have."

Jesus will say, "It's too late."

Herod will be there. He will look across the golden boulevard, and he will see John the Baptist, whose head he severed. He will say, "John, I'm sorry; I was deceived. Jesus, please let me in."

Jesus will say, "Depart from Me into everlasting torment."

Judas, who sold his Master for 30 pieces of silver, the price of a slave, will be there. He will see one of the foundations of that city where his name was to be inscribed. He will say, "I walked with You, Jesus. I talked with You. I saw You raise Lazarus from the dead. Forgive me."

But the justice of God's gavel will crash in his ears for all eternity, "Too late, too late, too late, too late."

The Bible says,

> **"...behold, now is the accepted time; behold, now is the day of salvation."**
>
> **2 Corinthians 6:2**

"He, that being often reproved hardeneth his neck, shall suddenly be destroyed, and that without remedy."

Proverbs 29:1

You have but one enemy and that is the clock on the wall. Every Sunday, all across the world, you can hear beautiful messages of silvery eloquence about Jesus coming out of the grave – but His resurrection is past and yours is yet to come.

In Ezekiel 3, God said that if I fail to warn the wicked man of his wicked deed and he dies in his wickedness, his blood will be required at my hand.

There will be those backsliders at the White Throne Judgment who at one time knew the power of Christ's resurrection, but they turned a cold heart and walked away from the things of God.

Some may say, "I've tried religion; I've tried to be good." That is not enough. The message of God's Word is clear. Jesus told Nicodemus, "You must be born again" (John 3:3).

Paul challenges us in the book of Romans, **"That if thou shalt confess with thy mouth the Lord Jesus, and shalt believe in thine heart that God hath raised him from the dead, thou shalt be saved" (Romans 10:9).**

If you are part of the first resurrection, then the second one will have no power over you.

"...serve the living and true God; And...wait for his Son from heaven, whom he raised from the dead, even Jesus, which delivered us from the wrath to come."

1 Thessalonians 1:9-10

Bow your knee now or bow your knee later.
You make the choice.

Endnotes

[1] Walter B. Knight, *Knight's Master Book of New Illustrations* (Grand Rapids: Eerdman's Printing Co., 1956), p. 563

[2] Pike, John. "The World at War" *GlobalSecurity.org.* (July 9, 2005). <http://www.globalsecurity.org/military/world/war/index.html> (April 26, 2006).

[3] "Sudan." *The World Fact Book.* (20 April, 2006). <www.cia.gov/cia/publications/factbook/geos/su.html#people> (April 26, 2006).

[4] "Graphs." *U.S. Geological Survey: National Earthquake Information Center.* (October 17, 2005). <http://neic.usgs.gov/neis/eqlists/graphs.html> (April 27, 2006).

Your Hope Tool Kit

**Here Are the Tools, the Spiritual Hammer
and Nails, You Need to Biblically
Repair and Restore the Hope
Plank in Your Life.**

I.   **The Rapture Is No Fairy Tale**

Jesus Promised That He Would Return

Luke 21:34   And take heed to yourselves, lest at any time your hearts be overcharged with surfeiting, and drunkenness, and cares of this life, and so that day come upon you unawares.

v. 35   For as a snare shall it come on all them that dwell on the face of the whole earth.

v. 36   Watch ye therefore, and pray always, that ye may be accounted worthy to escape all these things that shall come to pass, and to stand before the Son of man.

Jesus Will Descend From Heaven With a Shout

1 Thessalonians 4:16   For the Lord himself shall descend from heaven with a shout, with the voice of the archangel, and with the trump of God: and the dead in Christ shall rise first:

v. 17 Then we which are alive and remain shall be caught up together with them in the clouds, to meet the Lord in the air: and so shall we ever be with the Lord.

Those who have died in a saved condition will rise first, and then living believers will join them in the air.

II.   Reasons for the Rapture

To Reward the Saints

1 Thessalonians 4:13 But I would not have you to be ignorant, brethren, concerning them which are asleep, that ye sorrow not, even as others which have no hope.

v. 14 For if we believe that Jesus died and rose again, even so them also which sleep in Jesus will God bring with him.

To Collect His Church

To Raise Believing Saints from the Dead

1 Corinthians 15:53 For this corruptible must put on incorruption, and this mortal must put on immortality.

Philippians 3:20 For our conversation is in heaven; from whence also we look for the Saviour, the Lord Jesus Christ:

v. 21 Who shall change our vile body, that it may be fashioned like unto his glorious body, according to the working whereby he is able even to subdue all things unto himself.

III.   Who Will Go?

Those Who Are Saved

1 Corinthians 15:22 For as in Adam all die, even so in Christ shall all be made alive.

v. 23 But every man in his own order: Christ the firstfruits; afterward they that are Christ's at his coming.

Those Who Have Done Good

John 5:28 Marvel not at this: for the hour is coming, in the which all that are in the graves shall hear his voice,

v. 29 And shall come forth; they that have done good, unto the resurrection of life; and they that have done evil, unto the resurrection of damnation.

Those Without Stain or Spot

Ephesians 5:27 That he might present it to himself a glorious church, not having spot, or wrinkle, or any such thing; but that it should be holy and without blemish.

IV.   Time of the Rapture

No Man Knows the Day or Hour

Mark 13:32 But of that day and that hour knoweth no man, no, not the angels which are in heaven, neither the Son, but the Father.

Signs of the Times

Daniel 12:4 But thou, O Daniel, shut up the words, and seal the book, even to the time of the end: many shall run to and fro, and knowledge shall be increased.

Luke 21:11 And great earthquakes shall be in divers places, and famines, and pestilences; and fearful sights and great signs shall there be from heaven.

Luke 21:25 And there shall be signs in the sun, and in the moon, and in the stars; and upon the earth distress of nations, with perplexity; the sea and the waves roaring.

V.   The Second Advent

Perilous Times Will Come

2 Timothy 3:1 This know also, that in the last days perilous times shall come.

v. 2 For men shall be lovers of their own selves, covetous, boasters, proud, blasphemers, disobedient to parents, unthankful, unholy,

v. 3 Without natural affection, trucebreakers, false accusers, incontinent, fierce, despisers of those that are good,

v. 4 Traitors, heady, highminded, lovers of pleasures more than lovers of God;

v. 5 Having a form of godliness, but denying the power thereof: from such turn away.

v. 6 For of this sort are they which creep into houses, and lead captive silly women laden with sins, led away with divers lusts.

The Spirit of Antichrist Is in the World

1 John 2:18 Little children, it is the last time: and as ye have heard that antichrist shall come, even now are there many antichrists; whereby we know that it is the last time.

1 John 4:3 And every spirit that confesseth not that Jesus Christ is come in the flesh is not of God: and this is that spirit of antichrist, whereof ye have heard that it should come; and even now already is it in the world.

Revelation 20:7 And when the thousand years are expired, Satan shall be loosed out of his prison,

v. 8 And shall go out to deceive the nations which are in the four quarters of the earth, Gog, and Magog, to gather them together to battle: the number of whom is as the sand of the sea.

v. 9 And they went up on the breadth of the earth, and compassed the camp of the saints about, and the beloved city: and fire came down from God out of heaven, and devoured them.

v. 10 And the devil that deceived them was cast into the lake of fire and brimstone, where the beast and the false prophet are, and shall be tormented day and night for ever and ever.

VI.   The Millennial Growth of the Kingdom of God

Jesus Described the Kingdom in Parables

Matthew 13:31 Another parable put he forth unto them, saying, The kingdom of heaven is like to a grain of mustard seed, which a man took, and sowed in his field:

v. 32 Which indeed is the least of all seeds: but when it is grown, it is the greatest among herbs, and becometh a tree, so that the birds of the air come and lodge in the branches thereof.

Mark 4:26 And he said, So is the kingdom of God, as if a man should cast seed into the ground;

v. 27 And should sleep, and rise night and day, and the seed should spring and grow up, he knoweth not how.

v. 28 For the earth bringeth forth fruit of herself; first the blade, then the ear, after that the full corn in the ear.

v. 29 But when the fruit is brought forth, immediately he putteth in the sickle, because the harvest is come.

v. 30 And he said, Whereunto shall we liken the kingdom of God? or with what comparison shall we compare it?

v. 31 It is like a grain of mustard seed, which, when it is sown in the earth, is less than all the seeds that be in the earth:

v. 32 But when it is sown, it groweth up, and becometh greater than all herbs, and shooteth out great branches; so that the fowls of the air may lodge under the shadow of it.

Luke 13:18 Then said he, Unto what is the kingdom of God like? and whereunto shall I resemble it?

v. 19 It is like a grain of mustard seed, which a man took, and cast into his garden; and it grew, and waxed a great tree; and the fowls of the air lodged in the branches of it.

Daniel Foresaw It

Daniel 2:34 Thou sawest till that a stone was cut out without hands, which smote the image upon his feet that were of iron and clay, and brake them to pieces.

v. 35 Then was the iron, the clay, the brass, the silver, and the gold, broken to pieces together, and became like the chaff of the summer threshingfloors; and the wind carried them away, that no place was found for them: and the stone that smote the image became a great mountain, and filled the whole earth.

VII.   Universal Triumph of Christianity

All Nations Shall Come

Psalm 22:27 All the ends of the world shall remember and turn unto the Lord: and all the kindreds of the nations shall worship before thee.

A Seed Shall Serve Him

Psalm 22:30 A seed shall serve him; it shall be accounted to the Lord for a generation.

v. 31 They shall come, and shall declare his righteousness unto a people that shall be born, that he hath done this.

The House of the Lord Shall Be Established

Isaiah 2:2 And it shall come to pass in the last days, that the mountain of the Lord's house shall be established in the top of the mountains, and shall be exalted above the hills; and all nations shall flow unto it.

v. 3 And many people shall go and say, Come ye, and let us go up to the mountain of the Lord, to the house of the God of Jacob; and he will teach us of his ways, and we will walk in his paths: for out of Zion shall go forth the law, and the word of the Lord from Jerusalem.

v. 4 And he shall judge among the nations, and shall rebuke many people: and they shall beat their swords into plowshares, and their spears into pruninghooks: nation shall not lift up sword against nation, neither shall they learn war any more.

v. 5 O house of Jacob, come ye, and let us walk in the light of the Lord.

v. 6 Therefore thou hast forsaken thy people the house of Jacob, because they be replenished from the east, and are soothsayers like the Philistines, and they please themselves in the children of strangers.

v. 7 Their land also is full of silver and gold, neither is there any end of their treasures; their land is also full of horses, neither is there any end of their chariots:

v. 8 Their land also is full of idols; they worship the work of their own hands, that which their own fingers have made:

v. 9 And the mean man boweth down, and the great man humbleth himself: therefore forgive them not.

v. 10 Enter into the rock, and hide thee in the dust, for fear of the Lord, and for the glory of his majesty.

v. 11 The lofty looks of man shall be humbled, and the haughtiness of men shall be bowed down, and the Lord alone shall be exalted in that day.

v. 12 For the day of the Lord of hosts shall be upon every one that is proud and lofty, and upon every one that is lifted up; and he shall be brought low:

v. 13 And upon all the cedars of Lebanon, that are high and lifted up, and upon all the oaks of Bashan,

v. 14 And upon all the high mountains, and upon all the hills that are lifted up,

v. 15 And upon every high tower, and upon every fenced wall,

v. 16 And upon all the ships of Tarshish, and upon all pleasant pictures.

v. 17 And the loftiness of man shall be bowed down, and the haughtiness of men shall be made low: and the Lord alone shall be exalted in that day.

v. 18 And the idols he shall utterly abolish.

v. 19 And they shall go into the holes of the rocks, and into the caves of the earth, for fear of the Lord, and for the glory of his majesty, when he ariseth to shake terribly the earth.

Micah 4:1 But in the last days it shall come to pass, that the mountain of the house of the Lord shall be established in the top of the mountains, and it shall be exalted above the hills; and people shall flow unto it.

v. 2 And many nations shall come, and say, Come, and let us go up to the mountain of the Lord, and to the house of the God of Jacob; and he will teach us of his ways, and we will walk in his paths: for the law shall go forth of Zion, and the word of the Lord from Jerusalem.

All Nations Shall Fear the Lord

Micah 7:16 The nations shall see and be confounded at all their might: they shall lay their hand upon their mouth, their ears shall be deaf.

v. 17 They shall lick the dust like a serpent, they shall move out of their holes like worms of the earth: they shall be afraid of the Lord our God, and shall fear because of thee.

VIII. Universal Peace

Swords Into Plowshares

Isaiah 2:4 And he shall judge among the nations, and shall rebuke many people: and they shall beat their swords into plowshares, and their spears into pruninghooks: nation shall not lift up sword against nation, neither shall they learn war any more.

v. 5 O house of Jacob, come ye, and let us walk in the light of the Lord.

A Little Child Shall Lead Them

Isaiah 11:6 The wolf also shall dwell with the lamb, and the leopard shall lie down with the kid; and the calf and the young lion and the fatling together; and a little child shall lead them.

v. 7 And the cow and the bear shall feed; their young ones shall lie down together: and the lion shall eat straw like the ox.

v. 8 And the sucking child shall play on the hole of the asp, and the weaned child shall put his hand on the cockatrice' den.

v. 9 They shall not hurt nor destroy in all my holy mountain: for the earth shall be full of the knowledge of the Lord, as the waters cover the sea.

IX.   The End of Evil

The Binding of Satan

Revelation 20:1 And I saw an angel come down from heaven, having the key of the bottomless pit and a great chain in his hand.

v. 2 And he laid hold on the dragon, that old serpent, which is the Devil, and Satan, and bound him a thousand years,

v. 3 And cast him into the bottomless pit, and shut him up, and set a seal upon him, that he should deceive the nations no more, till the thousand years should be fulfilled: and after that he must be loosed a little season.

v. 4 And I saw thrones, and they sat upon them, and judgment was given unto them: and I saw the souls of them that were beheaded for the witness of Jesus, and for the word of God, and which had not worshipped the beast, neither his image, neither had received his mark upon their foreheads, or in their hands; and they lived and reigned with Christ a thousand years.

v. 5 But the rest of the dead lived not again until the thousand years were finished. This is the first resurrection.

v. 6 Blessed and holy is he that hath part in the first resurrection: on such the second death hath no power, but they shall be priests of God and of Christ, and shall reign with him a thousand years.

The Destruction of the Antichrist

2 Thessalonians 2:8 And then shall that Wicked be revealed, whom the Lord shall consume with the spirit of his mouth, and shall destroy with the brightness of his coming:

v. 9 Even him, whose coming is after the working of Satan with all power and signs and lying wonders,

v. 10 And with all deceivableness of unrighteousness in them that perish; because they received not the love of the truth, that they might be saved.

X. The Last Judgment

The Book of Life Is Opened

Revelation 20:12 And I saw the dead, small and great, stand before God; and the books were opened: and another book was opened, which is the book of life: and the dead were judged out of those things which were written in the books, according to their works.

Jesus Christ Is To Be the Judge

John 12:47 And if any man hear my words, and believe not, I judge him not: for I came not to judge the world, but to save the world.

v. 48 He that rejecteth me, and receiveth not my words, hath one that judgeth him: the word that I have spoken, the same shall judge him in the last day.

Everyone Judged According to His Works

1 Corinthians 3:12 Now if any man build upon this foundation gold, silver, precious stones, wood, hay, stubble;

v. 13 Every man's work shall be made manifest: for the day shall declare it, because it shall be revealed by fire; and the fire shall try every man's work of what sort it is.

v. 14 If any man's work abide which he hath built thereupon, he shall receive a reward.

v. 15 If any man's work shall be burned, he shall suffer loss: but he himself shall be saved; yet so as by fire.

The Second Death

Revelation 20:14 And death and hell were cast into the lake of fire. This is the second death.

XI.   New Heaven and New Earth

Creation Groans in Travail

Romans 8:19 For the earnest expectation of the creature waiteth for the manifestation of the sons of God.

v. 20 For the creature was made subject to vanity, not willingly, but by reason of him who hath subjected the same in hope,

v. 21 Because the creature itself also shall be delivered from the bondage of corruption into the glorious liberty of the children of God.

v. 22 For we know that the whole creation groaneth and travaileth in pain together until now.

We Look Forward to the New Heaven and New Earth

2 Peter 3:13 Nevertheless we, according to his promise, look for new heavens and a new earth, wherein dwelleth righteousness.

v. 14 Wherefore, beloved, seeing that ye look for such things, be diligent that ye may be found of him in peace, without spot, and blameless.

Revelation 21:1 And I saw a new heaven and a new earth: for the first heaven and the first earth were passed away; and there was no more sea.

Isaiah 65:17 For, behold, I create new heavens and a new earth: and the former shall not be remembered, nor come into mind.

XII.   The Blessings of Heaven

Salvation

1 Peter 1:9 Receiving the end of your faith, even the salvation of your souls.

Revelation 2:11 He that hath an ear, let him hear what the Spirit saith unto the churches; He that overcometh shall not be hurt of the second death.

Sinlessness

Revelation 14:5 And in their mouth was found no guile: for they are without fault before the throne of God.

Likeness to Christ

1 John 3:2 Beloved, now are we the sons of God, and it doth not yet appear what we shall be: but we know that, when he shall appear, we shall be like him; for we shall see him as he is.

Association With Christ

John 12:26 If any man serve me, let him follow me; and where I am, there shall also my servant be: if any man serve me, him will my Father honour.

2 Corinthians 5:6 Therefore we are always confident, knowing that, whilst we are at home in the body, we are absent from the Lord.

Reigning With Christ

Matthew 19:27 Then answered Peter and said unto him, Behold, we have forsaken all, and followed thee; what shall we have therefore?

v. 28 And Jesus said unto them, Verily I say unto you, That ye which have followed me, in the regeneration when the Son of man shall sit in the throne of his glory, ye also shall sit upon twelve thrones, judging the twelve tribes of Israel.

Revelation 3:21 To him that overcometh will I grant to sit with me in my throne, even as I also overcame, and am set down with my Father in his throne.

Revelation 22:5 And there shall be no night there; and they need no candle, neither light of the sun; for the Lord God giveth them light: and they shall reign for ever and ever.

The Vision of God

Revelation 22:3 And there shall be no more curse: but the throne of God and of the Lamb shall be in it; and his servants shall serve him.

v. 4 And they shall see his face; and his name shall be in their foreheads.

Perfect Knowledge

1 Corinthians 13:12 For now we see through a glass, darkly; but then face to face: now I know in part; but then shall I know even as also I am known.

Fullness of Glory and Joy

Revelation 21:4 And God shall wipe away all tears from their eyes; and there shall be no more death, neither sorrow, nor crying, neither shall there be any more pain: for the former things are passed away.

No More Sickness

Isaiah 33:24 And the inhabitant shall not say, I am sick: the people that dwell therein shall be forgiven their iniquity.

No More Hunger Nor Thirst

Revelation 7:15 Therefore are they before the throne of God, and serve him day and night in his temple: and he that sitteth on the throne shall dwell among them.

v. 16. They shall hunger no more, neither thirst any more; neither shall the sun light on them, nor any heat.

v. 17 For the Lamb which is in the midst of the throne shall feed them, and shall lead them unto living fountains of waters: and God shall wipe away all tears from their eyes.

We Will Eat of the Tree of Life

Luke 14:15 And when one of them that sat at meat with him heard these things, he said unto him, Blessed is he that shall eat bread in the kingdom of God.

Revelation 2:7 He that hath an ear, let him hear what the Spirit saith unto the churches; To him that overcometh will I give to eat of the tree of life, which is in the midst of the paradise of God.

Revelation 2:17 He that hath an ear, let him hear what the Spirit saith unto the churches; To him that overcometh will I give to eat of the hidden manna, and will give him a white stone, and in the stone a new name written, which no man knoweth saving he that receiveth it.

We Will Drink of the Water of Life

Revelation 21:6 And he said unto me, It is done. I am Alpha and Omega, the beginning and the end. I will give unto him that is athirst of the fountain of the water of life freely.

We Will Be Praising God

Revelation 2:3 And hast borne, and hast patience, and for my name's sake hast laboured, and hast not fainted.

Revelation 14:2 And I heard a voice from heaven, as the voice of many waters, and as the voice of a great thunder: and I heard the voice of harpers harping with their harps.

Revelation 15:1 And I saw another sign in heaven, great and marvellous, seven angels having the seven last plagues; for in them is filled up the wrath of God.

v. 2 And I saw as it were a sea of glass mingled with fire: and them that had gotten the victory over the beast, and over his image, and over his mark, and over the number of his name, stand on the sea of glass, having the harps of God.

v. 3 And they sing the song of Moses the servant of God, and the song of the Lamb, saying, Great and marvellous are thy works, Lord God Almighty; just and true are thy ways, thou King of saints.

v. 4 Who shall not fear thee, O Lord, and glorify thy name? for thou only art holy: for all nations shall come and worship before thee; for thy judgments are made manifest.

v. 5 And after that I looked, and, behold, the temple of the tabernacle of the testimony in heaven was opened.

We Will Have Eternal Life

Matthew 19:29 And every one that hath forsaken houses, or brethren, or sisters, or father, or mother, or wife, or children, or lands, for my name's sake, shall receive an hundredfold, and shall inherit everlasting life.

Romans 6:23 For the wages of sin is death; but the gift of God is eternal life through Jesus Christ our Lord.

Galatians 6:7 Be not deceived; God is not mocked: for whatsoever a man soweth, that shall he also reap.

v. 8 For he that soweth to his flesh shall of the flesh reap corruption; but he that soweth to the Spirit shall of the Spirit reap life everlasting.

GOD'S WORD

————————

**Restoring Biblical Doctrine
and Bible Preaching to the
Body of Christ**

————————

GOD'S WORD

Restoring Biblical Doctrine and Bible Preaching to the Body of Christ

But men ask, "How can you prove the Book is inspired?" I answered, "Because it inspires me."

— D.L. Moody
Way of Faith[1]

A Radiogram Answered

A Presbyterian youth from New Orleans was a naval "wireless" operator during the war. Early one morning, after a night on duty, he snatched a few minutes for his "Quiet Hour" when no message was going over, and he was reading the Twenty-third Psalm.

Suddenly the thought came to him to send the Psalm out over the water and see if any ship would take it up. He did, and as he sent the last word sixteen ships answered a wireless "Amen."

— Christian Life[2]

The Word Lives

Ingersoll held up a copy of the Bible and said, "In fifteen years, I'll have this book in the morgue."

Fifteen years rolled by, Ingersoll was in the morgue and the Bible lives on.

Voltaire said that in one hundred years the Bible would be an outmoded and forgotten book, to be found only in museums. When the one hundred years were up, Voltaire's house was owned and used by the Geneva Bible Society.

And recently ninety-two volumes of Voltaire's works – a part of the Earl of Derby's library – were sold for two dollars!

— Rev. Eugene M. Harrison
in Moody Monthly[3]

"…our God whom we serve is able to deliver us…"

Daniel 3:17

It is impossible to rightly govern the world without God and the Bible.

— George Washington[4]

A man was compelled one night to cross a wide, frozen river. Notwithstanding the assurances of those who were thoroughly familiar with the region and repeatedly crossed on the solid ice, the traveler feared to undertake the trip, but finally began to crawl his way over.

When near the middle of the frozen stream he was startled by a sound in the distance, and caught sight of a…[man] driving a heavy team of horses pulling a great load of pig iron; yet, there was not the least sign of a crack in the ice.

Will the Word of God hold?

Some fear to trust it.

Why, man, it can't fail!

— Sunday School Times[5]

The Anchoring Oak of God's Word

The key to rebuilding the bridge of truth across the chasm of sin is to have the anointed Word of God.

What I have revealed in this volume is nothing new. Oral Roberts stormed across platforms years ago with the same message. Dr. Lester Sumrall was casting out demons in the mountains of Tibet decades ago.

The message is not new, but it does represent a revival returning to the church – a revival to stop what we allowed the devil to steal out of our theology.

Thank God, we are going to put it back in and restore the glory to the body of Christ!

We are going to see our altars so lined with sinners seeking God that the preachers cannot do anything but direct them where to go!

This sounds simple, but it is God's answer to bring power and victory back to the Body of Christ. The greatest tool in God's tool chest to nail down all the truth of this book is simply this: the Word of God – the pure, powerful, unadulterated Word of the living God.

Would you like to go to your church this Sunday and hear more than a message from a monthly magazine? How about a message from the Word of Almighty God? How about a message served up fresh and hot, straight from the Holy Ghost?

Well, some say the Word's not relevant.

I declare it is the oak of God planted in the forests of eternity, entwining its roots around the rock of ages.

God said what He meant, and He meant what He said.

It is time we restored biblical doctrine and Bible preaching to the church – the infallibility and the inerrancy of the eternal edict of Almighty God.

"For ever, O Lord, thy word is settled in heaven."

Psalm 119:89

His Word is settled in heaven.

> **"For as the rain cometh down, and the snow from heaven, and returneth not thither, but watereth the earth, and maketh it bring forth and bud, that it may give seed to the sower, and bread to the eater:**
>
> **"So shall my word be that goeth forth out of my mouth: it shall not return unto me void, but it shall accomplish that which I please, and it shall prosper in the thing whereto I sent it."**
>
> **Isaiah 55:10-11**

That is a strange statement.

The Word, like the rain, comes down from heaven and does not return. The last part of that scripture seems contradictory. God says it does not return, but He then says "it will not return unto Me void, but will accomplish what it was sent to do."

How can it "not return" and then return victorious?

This scripture simply means that the only way God's Word will return to Him is as it is returned by our lips as we speak that Word from a heart filled with faith.

As we speak His Word, His purposes will be accomplished in our lives and in the world.

By releasing God's Word to work in the earth, we will be rebuilding the bridge between heaven and earth. We will become repairers of the breach and restorers of paths to dwell in.

Endnotes

[1] Walter B. Knight, *Knight's Master Book of New Illustrations* (Grand Rapids: Eerdman's Printing Co., 1956), p. 41

[2] *Ibid.*

[3] *Ibid.,* p. 29

[4] *Ibid.,* p. 27

[5] *Ibid.*

Your Bible Tool Kit

This Is the Key You Need To Securely Anchor All the Planks Into Your Life.

The Bible is a library of 66 books revealing God's divine plan for man. The Bible was written over a span of 1,500 years by over 40 authors from all walks of life. Although it was written on different continents and in different ages, all the books have become one book, which we know as the Bible.

I.   How the Bible Is Divided

The Bible is divided into two parts: The Old and New Testaments

Old Testament – 39 Books

Law or Books of Moses	*History*	*Poetry*
Genesis	Joshua	Job
Exodus	Judges	Psalms
Leviticus	Ruth	Proverbs
Numbers	1 Samuel	Ecclesiastes
Deuteronomy	2 Samuel	Song of Solomon
	1 Kings	
	2 Kings	
	1 Chronicles	
	2 Chronicles	
	Ezra	
	Nehemiah	
	Esther	

<u>*Major Prophets*</u>	<u>*Minor Prophets*</u>
Isaiah	Hosea
Jeremiah	Joel
Lamentations	Amos
Ezekiel	Obadiah
Daniel	Jonah
	Micah
	Nahum
	Habakkuk
	Zephaniah
	Haggai
	Zechariah
	Malachi

New Testament – 27 books

<u>*Gospels*</u>	<u>*History*</u>	<u>*Paul's Letters*</u>
Matthew	Acts	Romans
Mark		1 Corinthians
Luke		2 Corinthians
John		Galatians
		Ephesians
<u>*General Epistles*</u>		Philippians
Hebrews		Colossians
James		1 Thessalonians
1 Peter		2 Thessalonians
2 Peter		1 Timothy
1 John		2 Timothy
2 John		Titus
3 John		Philemon
Jude		

<u>*Prophecy*</u>
Revelation

II. Theme

The Bible has one central theme: the creation, the fall, and the redemption of the human race. This redemption was brought about by God through Jesus Christ and carried out by the Holy Spirit. The first three chapters of the Bible deal with the creation and fall of man, while the remainder deals with the restoration of man's relationship and fellowship with God.

III. How the Bible Was Written

God was actively involved in the recording of His Word. The Bible was not written simply because a man or group of men thought it would be a good idea.

We Know This Because of the Contents of the Bible

Good men would not write down what God said if they knew it was not God saying it.

Evil men would have never written anything to expose their sins and shortcomings.

Supernatural Aspects of the Bible Being Written

Inspiration literally means "God-breathed." It is the special power or influence upon the hearts and minds of writers of scripture which enabled them to make an infallible record of divine truth to men.

2 Timothy 3:16 All scripture is given by inspiration of God, and is profitable for doctrine, for reproof, for correction, for instruction in righteousness:

v. 17 That the man of God may be perfect, thoroughly furnished unto all good works.

2 Peter 1:21 ...holy men of God spake as they were moved [literally, borne along] by the Holy Ghost.

Revelation literally means to unveil, uncover or reveal. It is the uncovering of facts and truths which an individual could not know of himself, but are uncovered or revealed by the Spirit of God.

Galatians 1:11 But I certify you, brethren, that the gospel which was preached of me is not after man.

v. 12 For I neither received it of man, neither was I taught it, but by the revelation of Jesus Christ.

Revelation 1:1 The Revelation of Jesus Christ, which God gave unto him, to shew unto his servants things which must shortly come to pass; and he sent and signified it by his angel unto his servant John.

IV.   Benefits of the Word of God

Spirit and Life

John 6:63 It is the spirit that quickeneth; the flesh profiteth nothing: the words that I speak unto you, they are spirit, and they are life.

Health To Your Flesh

Proverbs 4:20 My son, attend to my words; incline thine ear unto my sayings.

v. 21 Let them not depart from thine eyes; keep them in the midst of thine heart.

v. 22 For they are life unto those that find them, and health to all their flesh.

A Light and Lamp

Psalm 119:105 Thy word is a lamp unto my feet, and a light unto my path.

Bread To Eat (food for your spirit)

Matthew 4:4 But he answered and said, It is written, Man shall not live by bread alone, but by every word that proceedeth out of the mouth of God.

1 Peter 2:2 As newborn babes, desire the sincere milk of the word, that ye may grow thereby.

Hebrews 5:14 But strong meat belongeth to them that are of full age, even those who by reason of use have their senses exercised to discern both good and evil.

Truth

John 17:17 Sanctify them through thy truth: thy word is truth.

Power To Deliver

Romans 1:16 For I am not ashamed of the gospel of Christ: for it is the power of God unto salvation to every one that believeth; to the Jew first, and also to the Greek.

Sword of the Spirit

Ephesians 6:17 And take the helmet of salvation, and the sword of the Spirit, which is the word of God.

V.   How To Approach Bible Reading and Study

Prayerfully

Ask God to open the eyes of your understanding to receive from His Word.

Faithfully

Reading God's Word should be a regular part of your life.

Proverbs 18:14 The spirit of a man will sustain his infirmity; but a wounded spirit who can bear?

Expectantly

God wants you to know His will for your life.

Have a right concept of the God who spoke His Word. He is a good God who wants good things for His children.

Matthew 7:11 If ye then, being evil, know how to give good gifts unto your children, how much more shall your Father which is in heaven give good things to them that ask him?

As you read and study God's Word, allow it to change you. The Bible is a Christian's absolute standard of faith and conduct. It is the measure by which your life will be judged. Never try to change the Word to fit your life, but allow it to change you to conform to God's standards. As you do so, you will be washed, cleansed from the lusts of the world, and sanctified as a vessel unto honor.

Ephesians 5:26 That he might sanctify and cleanse it with the washing of water by the word.

My Blessing Upon You

You have come to the Kingdom of God for such a time as this. This is your hour, your day, your opportunity for divine destiny – to cause the Word of God to be fulfilled and the scripture to declare, "These that have turned the world upside down are come here also."

So I bless you now.

I bless you beyond myself.

I bless you beyond the capacity of human limitation.

I dig deep within me to the anointing which resides and abides forever, and I release that anointing upon you from the crown of your head to the soles of your feet.

You have spent your last ordinary moment.

I command your perception of the world to be seen through the focus of the blood of the cross of Christ.

I mark you now by that cross. Even as our Savior bears those marks, so you are changed this moment. Changed, to bear God's mark.

I mark you with the anointing of God. You will see as God sees and hear as God hears.

You will receive an insatiable hunger and desire for the courts of your God, and none of the pabulum of this earth will satisfy your craving – for you are hungry and thirsty for your God.

I create within you a chasm that can only be filled by the flooding presence of the Holy Ghost.

Hunger for Him.

Thirst for Him.

Fight under Him and crown Him Lord of all.

Now, I bless you.

I release you from the fear of your past, the fear of your present, and from the fear of your future.

I release you into the very bosom of the God who created this world and stuck a cross in the middle of it and hung His Son on it for your deliverance. May you know Him as no person has ever known Him, and may everywhere you go the tongued witness of the people declare, "The people of God are among us."

Now it is time to press forward, forgetting those things which are behind.

May this be your prayer, **"I press toward the mark for the prize of the high calling of God in Christ Jesus" (Philippians 3:14).**

Amen.

About the Author

ROD PARSLEY, bestselling author of more than sixty books, is the dynamic pastor of World Harvest Church in Columbus, Ohio, a church with worldwide ministries and a global outreach. As a highly sought-after crusade and conference speaker whom God has raised up as a prophetic voice to America and the world, Parsley is calling people to Jesus Christ through the good news of the Gospel.

He oversees Bridge of Hope Missions, Harvest Preparatory School, World Harvest Bible College, and the *Breakthrough* broadcast, a television and radio show seen by millions and broadcast to nearly 200 countries around the world, including a potential viewing audience of 97% of the homes in the United States and 78% in Canada. *Breakthrough* is carried on 1,400 stations and cable affiliates, including the Trinity Broadcasting Network, the Canadian Vision Network, Armed Forces Radio and Television Network, and in several countries spanning the globe.

Parsley's refreshingly direct style encourages Christians to examine and eradicate sin from their lives. A fearless champion of living God's way, Parsley follows the high standard set by Jesus Christ and compels his readers to do the same. He and his wife Joni have two children, Ashton and Austin.

OTHER BOOKS BY ROD PARSLEY

Ancient Wells, Living Water

At the Cross, Where Healing Begins

Could It Be?

The Day Before Eternity

He Came First

It's Already There

No Dry Season (Bestseller)

No More Crumbs (Bestseller)

On the Brink (#1 Bestseller)

Silent No More

For more information about *Breakthrough*,
World Harvest Church, World Harvest Bible College,
Harvest Preparatory School,
The Center for Moral Clarity, or to receive a product list of the
many books, CDs and DVDs by Rod Parsley, write or call:

Breakthrough/World Harvest Church
P.O. Box 32932
Columbus, OH 43232-0932 USA
(614) 837-1990 (Office)
www.breakthrough.net

World Harvest Bible College
P.O. Box 32901
Columbus, OH 43232-0901 USA
(614) 837-4088
www.worldharvestbiblecollege.org

Harvest Preparatory School
P.O. Box 32903
Columbus, OH 43232-0903 USA
(614) 837-1990
www.harvestprep.org

The Center for Moral Clarity
P.O. Box 32903
Columbus, OH 43232-9926 USA
(613) 382-1188
www.CenterForMoralClarity.net

If you need prayer, Breakthrough Prayer Warriors are ready to pray
with you 24 hours a day, 7 days a week at: (800) 424-8644